SO-EFO-659

Religious Poems
and
Testimonies

by...Merlene Howard

authorHOUSE™

1663 LIBERTY DRIVE, SUITE 200
BLOOMINGTON, INDIANA 47403
(800) 839-8640
WWW.AUTHORHOUSE.COM

© 2005 Merlene Howard. All Rights Reserved.

No part of this book may be reproduced, stored in a retrieval system, or transmitted by any means without the written permission of the author.

First published by AuthorHouse 11/30/05

ISBN: 1-4208-9003-4 (sc)

Printed in the United States of America
Bloomington, Indiana

This book is printed on acid-free paper.

To all of my grandchildren, and especially Tanika,
the first to read and edit this book. I love you all
Nana

Chapter 1

My name is Merlene Howard, and today I am so blessed. It's January and God has let me see another New Year. Some did not make it. A friend of mine is being buried today, and I would like to dedicate this poem to her. It is called, "To live is Christ."

To Live is Christ

To live is Christ, what a wonderful life
And to die is gain
I'll celebrate a heavenly day
With no more sorrow and no pain

I'll walk in heaven on streets of gold
Where there are treasures untold
But while I live here on this earth
Reaching sinners is my goal

I'll tell them of the life in Christ
And I'll tell them until I die
So they may know how sweet it is
And of our home up in the sky

One day you'll call my name and
I will already be gone
Until that day, I'll tell the world
Until Jesus calls me home

Since we know not the time, or the place, when God will call us home, it's time to get our lives right with Him. God has no respected person, he calls the young, as well as the old. Sometimes without warning. You don't have to be on your sick bed to be called, it's time to get ready.

Are You ready?
A woman died at age 102
And another at forty seven
That same day, a man of twenty-one
And a child of just eleven

It's time you get to thinking
Am I ready to meet my maker?
If Jesus should come tomorrow
Would I be the one who's taken?

Everyone should live every minute
As though it were our last
Will tomorrow be our future
Or will it be our past?

It doesn't matter much
What was the year of your birth
God decides young and old
Who's being taken from this Earth

So when a hurricane, or earthquake
Begin to shake your home
Think, it might be Jesus returning
And He's shaking them old bones

So, are you ready?
Are you a saint or a sinner?
You sure can't be both
so live to be a winner
Are You Ready?

We all know, when we are born, one day we will die. So we must decide our destiny. Where do we want to spend eternity? In heaven or in hell? Ask yourself as this next poem asks, "Do you wanna go to heaven?"

Do you wanna go to heaven?

Do you wanna go to heaven
Where the streets are paved with gold?
Where the treasures surround you
And riches are untold

The kingdom of heaven is like a treasure
Or like fine choice pearls
Angels will separate the wicked from the godly
At the end of the world

Stop! There's no use weeping
Don't you understand?
Get your life right with Jesus
Before you're taken from this land

Every soul on Earth has
A choice of where to go
To heaven to live with Jesus
Or to hell down below
(Matt. 10:70)

Now let us celebrate this new year with a new life. A new life in Christ! Call Him, He will answer. Remember, *God loves you!*

Chapter 2

A life with Christ

Do you know, there are people today, living a life of stress and worry? Going to bed crying, waking up so stressed out they can't think straight? Well, that's the devils plan, and he's working it. It's your reward for choosing him over Jesus. Jesus is the light of the world. He told us to "Let not our hearts be troubled" (John 14:1-3). He tells us to believe in Him, and also the Father. He is preparing a place for us, in heaven, and worry and stress will not get us there.

Sometimes we have to search, our past to see what brought us to this point, then we must do what we have to do to get us out of that situation. You gave your heart to God, and was given by Him, outstanding blessings. You know they came from Him, (your testimony). Still you turn your back, and return to a sinful world, where you have found out that nothing works any more. Your so-called friends are gone, who's got your back now? The alcohol, or the crack pipe? Maybe that sweet talking honey, that talked you into sex out of wedlock, and left you pregnant, or with aids. Or you find you are no longer shouting for Jesus, but you are shouting and fighting in the streets. What is so appealing about that life, over a life of peace with Jesus. It's not always smooth sailing, but when you wake up in the middle of the night, you can call on His great name

Jesus will supply your needs, when you give yourself whole hearty, to Him. You see, the joy of the Lord is righteousness, and peace. With God in your heart, even on your bad days, you can have joy. Believe me, joy can overcome, all your stress. I was listening to a TV. evangelist one morning, and she said, sometimes you have to laugh your way out.

(Proverbs 17:22) says, a merry heart is like medicine, but a broken spirit dries the bones. Trust God, and you can laugh again. Trust Him, He did it before and He can do it again. If you let the cares of the world overcome you, and break your spirit, they will cause you to lose your life. If you wallow in stress, it can only get worst. Jesus said don't worry, let Him handle it. (Matt 6:25-34).

It may be to big for us to handle, but not for our father. Give it to him and live again.

Worry

Wait on the Lord
Wait on Him O I say
These are the words of David
And they mean a lot today

Patience is a virtue
And worry is a sin
Give your heart to the Savior
Let Jesus take them in

The Lord will never fail us
No, he never does
Trust the Lord forever
And forget what worry was

Now, I ask you, is giving up sin, to serve the Lord, really such a great sacrifice? Are you giving up stuff that you really want to hold on to? Are you holding on to some little sins, and refusing to give them up? Is there anything in your life that has the world saying, "Did you see that?" I knew he or she wasn't saved. As saved people, *we are different,* we have to come away from worldly things, (1 John 2:15-16). We must walk in the life of Christ Jesus. The more you try to walk like Him, the more you want to give up sin, and be like Him. Put on God's whole armor. You are in a fight against the rules of darkness and spiritual evil, (Eph. 6:10-20).

God's Whole Armor

Put on God's whole armor
If you choose to fight this fight
To stand against the devil
You must be strong in God's might

Having your loins girt about with truth
And a breastplate of righteousness
You feet shod in the gospel, of peace
And then put on the rest

Above all take the shield of faith
So you can quench all fiery darts
With you breastplate and your shield
You will protect your loving heart

Then take your helmet of salvation
Along with a sword of God's word
Praying always in the spirit
Now tell the world what you just heard

The armor of God covers our front from head to toe, and God has our backs. With God on our side, we are winners, for without Him we are nothing.

Without God I Am Nothing

Without God I am nothing
Just flesh without a soul
Just another sinner, sinning
Like we came from the same mold

If I open my mouth without Him
There's no telling what will come out
A whole lot of rambling nothings
Fear, distrust, and doubt
But, oh with Christ within me
There's nothing I can't do
If I just let Him lead me
He will lead me through

I just have to praise Him
then praise Him some more
My God is so worthy
It's Him that I adore

So come now and join me
Give God the highest praise
Hallelujah, Christ my savior
Help me to always walk in your ways

With God in my life, I smile more. I want to do random acts of kindness all the time. I don't get angry, when I speak to someone who doesn't speak back to me, I just try again the next time I see them. There's no room for stress in my life, Jesus and mine. I can be the first to say, I'm sorry, even when I feel I'm not wrong, (that's a hard one for me) but I can do it, Jesus and me. We can ask for forgiveness and forgive others, Jesus and me. Let Jesus lead you, and you can't go wrong. Learn to follow and listen, He never fails.

WITH JESUS IN MY LIFE

With Jesus in my life there's
No room for sin and stress
With Jesus in my life
I have an urge to do my best

He will never leave me
There's no doubt this is true
I know if He said it
He'll do what He said he would do

When I am weak
As often it seems that I am
He picks me up, for He's so strong
Yet, gentle as a lamb

With Jesus in my life
There's just no room for sin
With Jesus in my life
I have a true blue friend

I thank God for these wonderful poems. They are truly uplifting. He covers all thing in my life. They help me and I hope they do the same for you. If you are lost step out on Jesus. He won't let you down, try Him and see what he has in store for you. All you have to do is give Him praise.

GIVE HIM PRAISE

Give praise to Him all ye saints
Give thanks to his Holy name
His favor last for all our lives
And His anger is no game

Weeping may go on all night
But with morning there is joy
Saints give God all due respect
Remember He's no toy

Beg, beg, beg, my friends
If that is what it will take
Do whatever you have to do
To get into heavens gate

The enemy is busy, he
Gives us lots of woes
You can overcome them all
If you walk where Jesus goes

Jesus is a safety net
In Him you are strong
Commit your life to the Lord
He will not leave you alone
(Psalms 30)

Chapter 3

I'd like to bring a subject up, that comes up in conversation sometimes. It is *waiting.* as we reach our sixties, seventies, and eighty, (Yes it is quiet common these days) we look around and most of our friends and love one are gone. Some have passed on, some have moved in with family, some have been moved into convalescent homes. It's a natural process of life, or "old age." When you stop to look at life, you'll find it's a blessing to make it to old age. So many don't make it. It's sad to think of the fact, that sin has taken so, so, many, young and old.

Sins like aids, gang shooting, drugs, and alcohol. It's so sad, because God can save you from all those sins. All you have to do is ask. I'm not saying if you get saved, we will not die of these things, I'm saying, the body may be lost, but God can save the soul. Innocent people are sometimes caught up and lose their lives too. But we can still be forgiven of all our sins, and be set free, to live a life in Christ.

Ask Jesus to forgive your sins, He has forgiven murders. Still there are those that will not ask, and they die in sin. There are still others who feel that they still have time, they go to sleep, and never wake up again. *Oops,* times up!

There are still others, that live to be older or make it to "old age," and still can't call His name. Some suffer from senility, or Alzheimer's and can't remember how to pray and who to pray to.

My mother suffered from Alzheimer's. She was a woman of God who forgot a lot. But she would still, praise God and worship at church. I wrote this for her.

To my mom: Lillie Mae Johnson
1919-2000

It started real slow, I forgot a name
Then the favorite dish I cooked
Just didn't taste the same
I put on my shoe, on today, and I forgot my sock

It seems I can't remember
How to put a key in the lock

Today I can't remember, how to bait my hook
I can't sign my name, or
Read the good book

What's the matter with me?
Please tell me what's wrong
I can't seem to do anything, any more
At least, not on my own
Alzheimer's has taken over me
I can't remember the person
that I used to be

But I still remember, Jesus Christ
And his sweet , sweet, love
He will take care of me
My heavenly Father up above

God is worth your time, young and old. Oh what a life, if you live it in Christ. God has something for you at all ages….Don't wait.

I heard someone say, the other day
"The world has been ending for a hundred years"
I've seen the signs of times
He ain't came yet, so I have no fears

Well, if Jesus don't come for a hundred more
You won't be around to open your door
When He calls the dead up from the grave
Will you arise from where you are lay?

Don't wait until tomorrow to do your deeds
Work, work, for Jesus, it's Him you must please
So when the world does come to an end
You've done your God's work
And stayed away from sin

Now let me tell you brother
Your end on Earth is truly near
Tomorrow is promised to no man
So get your soul right with Jesus
And do it while you can

Don't wait until it's too late, saying I'm too young. The young die too. Take this chance to ask God to save you. Salvation belongs to the Lord….(Ps.3:8). When God saves you He gives you a testimony. Even if you never did drug, or had an affair, etc., you still have sin, to be delivered from. (1 John 1:8) says; we deceive ourselves if we say we have no sin, (1 John 1:7) tells us, the blood of Jesus cleansed us from all sin. God has something for you at all ages, you like Nicodemus can be born again.

"Born again"

"Can I enter my mother's womb again?"
Nicodemus asked our Lord
That's not the way to be born again
No, that would be too hard

If you want to be born again
You have to ask from on your knees
God's grace will be given you
For it's God you must please

This man came to Jesus by night
This ruler of the Jews
To hear Jesus teach, for he had heard
Of His good news

Do not marvel that I said to you
That you must be born again
To see the kingdom of the heaven
You must give up your sins

If I tell you of earthly things
And you do not believe
Then if I tell you of heavenly things
You most certainly will not receive

Don't wait, call on Jesus, before it's too late.

I want to talk a little more, about being born again. Nicodemus, thought right away of entering his mother's womb again, because he had never heard of being born again. He was an intelligent man, and he wasn't trying to be funny. He had never heard of being born again. He had never been taught like we have.

What? You say you've never been taught? Well, let me tell you a story. We know that once we have been born, we can't reenter our mother's womb again and start from scratch. Although with some of our children's lives they lead, with the first birth, maybe moms wish she could start again. But the pain I remember from child birth, (thanks to Eve) I wouldn't jump right into it, I'd have to think about it. A long time!

Then there is cloning. If at first you don't succeed, try, try again. But with cloning you are reproducing the same person over and over again. That may not be the best idea. We're trying to get rid of that old life, right? Being born again means we can get rid of old flesh and start anew. Jesus shed His blood on Calvary so we could be assured of that.

In St. John 3rd chapter, when Jesus said to Nicodemus, a man cannot see the kingdom of heaven, unless he is born again, He wasn't telling him to do the impossible, (although all things are possible with Jesus), no He wasn't telling him to reenter his mother's womb, He was telling him, he must enter into, and be born of the Holy Spirit.

Now the Holy Spirit isn't floating around like a ghostly figure you see in the movies, that you can snatch down and engulf yourself in, he doesn't work like that. Jesus described him as; *what is born of the flesh is flesh, and which is born of spirit is spirit. The wind blow where it wishes, you hear the sound, but can't tell where it comes from or where it is going. So is one born of the Holy Spirit.*

We know that the Holy Ghost comes from God, we just don't know how He gets Him to us. And just because He come in, it doesn't mean He has to stay. He cannot abide in an unclean temple. Wait a minute, I'm not talking about the Holy Spirit right now, I'm talking about being born again. In (John 1:12-13), God gives every man the right to become His child. You can be an heir.

BE AN HEIR

Jesus adopted me into the
Royal family one day
He said leave your sins and
Join me, I want you to stay

Come be my mother,
Brother and sister too
You can be royal, children
Because I love you

Come and join us sinner
I can hear you whine
Join the royal family
Don't be left behind

You are heirs to the kingdom
Put on your beautiful purple robe
Put your jeweled crown upon your head
And walk on streets of gold

The cattle on a thousand hills
As heirs belong to us
All we have to do to receive it
Is have faith, love and trust

Did you hear me sinner
We can be joint heirs with Christ
If we suffer with Him
We may also be glorified

We have the right to be born, not of blood and flesh, but of the will of God. In 1st Peter 2:23, it tells us of being born of incorruptible seed, through the word of God, which lives and abides forever. We are new creatures, and as a result, old things pass away; behold, all things have become new. (2 Cor. 5:17).

Just as new born babies constantly crave milk, we have a desire, a constant desire for a bottle of milk, the pure milk of the *Word*. (1 Peter 2:2)

God wants us to desire the word of God, with the same intensity, that babies want milk. Now, that don't mean you have to act like babies in all things, like it's your way or no way, your way may not be God's way. Listen and learn. Even old saints constantly need God's milk. For whatever is born of God, overcomes the world. When we become born again, our faith makes us strong. Strong to defeat weakness, bitterness, complaining, and other sins. Strong because we know that whosoever is born of God, does not sin; and the wicked one does not touch him. (1 John 5:18). We have to know we are of God, and all the evil around us, can't touch us.

So all you new, born-again Christian babies, live in the world, but not of the world. Live in the Word, read it, learn it, speak it, memorize it, and most of all live it. In everything you do, the Word will set you free. God gave His only Begotten Son, to die, because He loved us so much, and all we have to do is believe on Him. (John 3:16). So believe and eternal life can begin right now. You must be born again!

Once you are born again, you'll find it's so good to be God's child.

SO GOOD TO BE GOD'S CHILD

You can't get so low, that he won't forgive
For you are God's child
He sent His son to die , so we might live
So good to be God's child

Jesus is my brother,
My father, and my friend
He gave His life upon the cross
He died for all our sins
I know I can call Him anytime
For His love will never end
So good to be God's child

His love is so sweet and real
I want everyone, to feel what I feel
Sometime I want to jump and shout
Sometime I want to cry
I always want to praise His name
And I'll praise Him until I die
So good to be God's child

Chapter 4

A weak link

My granddaughter Danielle, and my grandson Khaneal, like to play a game with me, that we copied from the game show. When we see each other or talk on the phone, the first to say, "You're the weakest link" wins. It's very important to Khaneal, (age 7), to win every time, so he's not the weakest link. He works hard at being first. Well, we saints can take a lesson from Khaneal, and work hard at not being the weak link in God's chain.

I've often heard, a chain is as strong, as it's weakest link. Meaning if you have a flaw in a link, there is where the break will come. Jesus tells us, *"If your hand or foot causes you to sin, cut it off and cast it away, for it is better to be maimed then to be thrown into the fires of hell."(Matt. 18:8).*

Are you walking around, claiming to be of God, with a big flaw stamped in your forehead? The next poem is called,

"Weak Link"

I'm holding on trying to be strong
I don't want to be a weak link
I'm trusting in God to show me the way
For it's important to me what He thinks

I'm trying all I know how
To do what He said I must do
Jesus said to feed His sheep
And I'm getting the word out to you

His word is so wide
You can't to get around
And it's so deep
You can't go underground

We must preach, teach, and pray
Everywhere we go
Getting God's word out
On mountains high and valleys low

I've gotten a hold to a
Very strong chain
I won't be the weak link
For in me Jesus Christ reigns

If you're not working for Jesus, and feeding His sheep, you are a weak link. If you are not fasting, tithing, and worshipping Him, you are a weak link. If you are not working for Him, you have a flaw, so get to work, work for Jesus.

Work for Jesus

I am not a preacher, and neither can I sing
But I can pray to God and play the tambourine
I know as a saint of God's I have a job to do
And you as a saint of God have work to do too

We must live a life that others may see
That we are indeed Christ-like
And we must sow His seed

There's a job for everyone, saints get to work
Sing, pray, teach, or just clean the church
There's always something for all of us to do
Work, work for Jesus, let His love shine through you

When Jesus left, he told his disciples to feed His sheep (John 21:15-17). Three times Jesus told Simon Peter, to feed His sheep. We too are his disciples, are we feeding His sheep? We all have a job to do for God. When we say "I can't," "I don't know how," or just plain "No" we break the chain. Sometime we don't want the menial jobs, we want to be the leader, the head, the Pastor, and nothing else. Not good! There are so many jobs to do.

When you take all the jobs, or links, in the chain, put them together, you start with a leader, and with each added link, the chain grows longer. Then when you weld them together, working in unison, you can't tell where the chain began.

It's up to you to keep your link strong. To hold your link together, so the chain can't break there. In a chain you are not alone. You not only have the strength of the other links, you have the main link, Jesus and the Holy

Spirit, to keep your link strong. The chain must start with a leader, but with each link added the chain grows longer and stronger, until we are all a strong, long chain. So pull your weight, be strong in the word, live your life in Christ, hold on.

I remember a game we used to play as children, everyone would hold hands in a line, and form a chain. Then the other team would send their strongest person over to break through your chain. He would, (just like Satan) look for the weakest one in the chain to break through. I remember my older brother, helping me to hold on so he couldn't get through me. That's working together to make the chain strong.

Satan is looking for that weak spot in God's chain, and he will continue to hit there until he breaks through. Don't be that weak link, go to your back- up, prayer, and each other. He has no power, hold on. God's got your back. And when the battle is over God will say well done.

Well Done

Well done, thy good and faithful servant
You have been faithful over a few
I will make you ruler over many
For I see what you can do

Enter into the joy of the Lord

Lord, I had two talents, now I have four
Well done, thy good and faithful servant
you shall rule many more

Enter into the joy of the Lord

Lord, I Had but one, and
buried it in the ground
I kept it for myself didn't have
Enough to go around

Thy wicked, lazy servant
You shall reap what you sow
Give back what I have given you
For you I will not know

There shall be weeping and gashing of teeth
(Matt. 25:14-30)

Chapter 5

When did we get to the point that we can't pray for ourselves? Why is it only a famous TV preacher can heal us? (I believe that God has anointed some with the gift of healing, both on TV and off). Jesus told His disciples to go forth and heal the sick (Matt. 10-8). TV certainly can reach out a lot farther. But when did we stop praying for ourselves?

When was the last time your own Pastor had to leave his home in the middle of the night, or his job to come pray for something you could have just bowed down and prayed for yourself? Is Sunday prayer line the only time God hears prayer requests? How many of us have a prayer closet? How many of us still use it? (Matt. 6:6)

I believe the answer to all these questions is God. God is the healer, no matter who does the asking. God hears every prayer, no matter from where or when it comes. God hears every request and our faith, and belief in Him heals us. And isn't it wonderful how He hears all of us at once? He doesn't hear me for ten or fifteen minutes, than go and listen to you, He hears us all at once, all over the World. What a mighty God we serve.

Fight The Battle

Pray without ceasing
Put your whole armor on
God will lead us into battle
He never leaves us alone

You won't need guns and knifes
To fight with, no such things as these
You need to call on Jesus
Call Him from down on your knees

He gave us the Holy Spirit
Along with peace, joy, and love
With the fruit of the spirit in us
We are as gentle as a dove

God makes us ready for battle
We must get ready for the fight
Satan will come after us
That old devil just ain't right

Last week I had a really, really, bad headache. (it came from the epidermal shot I had in my back). It went on for a couple of days. I called my doctor, (didn't call Jesus), the doctor gave me a pain prescription that didn't touch the pain. I'm really hurting now. Finally it got so *bad* I called my sister to pray for me, but couldn't reach her. I had already called my Pastor and couldn't reach him. *Pain!* I think God was trying to tell me something.

Call On Jesus

Are you caught up in sin, like a bug in a web?
Struggling with all of your might to be free?
Make it easy on yourself, call on the Lord
Call Him from down on your knees

Sin is a struggle that sometimes seems
As if you can never be free
Kick it out of your life, call on Christ
He will be there just wait and see

Call on Jesus oh you sinner
Through Him is heaven's treasures
Oh what a life in the bosom of Christ
I want to live there forever

He's in the business of saving souls
And I know he sure saved me
Lay down sin, call on the Lord
Only God can set you free

This wonderful feeling you get when
You're saved, the joy is so sweet and good
Give up to Jesus you've got it made
Like you never thought you could

Finally, I got the message, I prayed for myself! I keep blessed oil in my home, but I wasn't using it. What was it there for? You see, I know what God can do! He has done so much for me already. So many times, and in so many ways. In finance, (I bought a house with bad credit) in healing, I've even prayed gas into my car (with today's prices, we need to all be praying). I don't know why I suffered so long without praying for myself. You have to be able to pray for yourself, before you can pray for others. Believe for yourself, then you can spread that belief to others. How can I tell you what God can do, when there is so much wrong with me? In Matthews 7:7 it says; *"Ask and it shall be given you, seek, and you shall find; knock and it shall be opened."* It also says in the 11th verse; *"My heavenly Father gives good things to those who ask."* Don't wait until you get sick, to ask for something from God, He wants us to have the very best of everything, after all, we are His children. He wants His children to live in the best of health, in the finest of houses, to have the best churches, drive the best cars, do well in business, just ask. Sometimes we have to go through some things, but the rewards are the best. Paul had his thorn in the flesh, that he asked to be removed, but God said; *My grace is sufficient for you…(2 Cor. 12:7-8).*

It may not come that very day, or even that year, but it's coming. It may not come easy, many blessings come with a battle. You must put on your whole armor, praying, always in the Spirit (Isa. 59:17)(Eph. 6:10-17). We can't let Satan bluff us. You remember the story of David and Goliath? Because of his size, Goliath, didn't have to fight. He just yelled real loud and bluffed. He had Saul's army shaking in their boots. But one day, a lad called David came by to bring his brother food. He heard Goliath's insults. Well, David, took offense to a great, big, old Philistine should insult his God's armies. You know the story, David called his bluff, with a sling and a rock, and God's anointing, David put him away. The bigger he was the harder, he fell. So don't let Satan bluff you, you have God on your side. God gives us the power. The power is the Word. And the Word will knock satan out. So pray for yourself, God hears you. Day and night, 24 hours. Pray, worship, and fast, fast, pray, and worship. Remember God has your back.

Chapter 6

Obeying

I want to talk to you about obeying. Trusting God in all things, and obey Him when He speaks.

"OBEY"

I was always a stubborn child
And just would not obey
Saying "no" to most everything
For I thought that was the way

As I grew older I
Became a stubborn teen
I was still a disobedient child
Some said I was just mean

But God came into my life one day
And I began to pray
I found that I could love the Lord
And I could then obey

I begin to live in His Word
And to teach it too
For when you love the Lord
You do as He says do

I will always love the Lord
And His will I will obey
I am now an obedient child
For God showed me the way

God tells me in His Word and
Now I am telling you
Live a long life in Christ
As the Word tells you too

Children obey your parents in the Lord, for this is right. Honor your father, and thy mother, which is the first commandment, with promise, that it may be well with thee, and thou mayest live long on earth. (Eph. 6:1-3).

Obey; the dictionary says; to carry out the orders of; to be guided by; to be obedient.

When I was a child, we were taught not only to obey our parents, and our teachers, but our elders period. That was out of respect for them. And if we obey the bible, we would still be obeying them today. God wants an obedient people. We *must* obey God. He is our father, and we must obey Him. We must obey our parents, and it's up to them to teach us, and to lead us to know, and obey God.

Disobedience can lead to lots of trouble, just ask Adam and Eve, or Jonah. Sooner or later our sin of disobedience will catch up with us. Jonah found out, you can run but you can't hide.

The Lord told Jonah to rise and go to Nineveh, a great and wicked city, to preach. But Jonah ran the other way, toward a city called Tarshish. He disobeyed God's calling, and ran from his ministry. He found a ship going to Tarshish, paid his fare, and went deep down within it. no doubt trying to hide.(You can't hide from God). But God said no! He sent a great wind, that tossed that boat, until it was about to be broken up. But old Jonah had went down as deep as he could go, and had fallen asleep. After the Captain figured out the storm was because of him, they tossed him into the sea. God had prepared a big fish to swallow Jonah, and he lay in the fishes belly for three days and three nights. Jonah began to pray. He repented, and the Lord had the big fish to vomit Jonah onto dry land. He preached at Nineveh and the people believed.

Jonah

"Arise, go to Nineveh," said the Lord
But Jonah , he wouldn't go
You'll just forgive them of their
Wickness, this I do know

I'll flee to Tarhish from God's presence
He found a ship and paid his fare
Down he went into the bottom
Like God couldn't find him there

A storm rose up, and scared the Captain
Poor Jonah they cast a lot on him
They then threw him into the sea
Jonah I hope you can swim

The Lord prepared a great fish
To swallow Jonah, in his belly he did sit
Jonah prayed and he repented
So God made the big fish spit

Back on land he preached at Nineveh
Said what God told him to say
And the Lord blessed the people
It had to be God's way

I know you are merciful, and slow to anger
One who relents from doing harm
It makes me so very angry
Now I wish I had not been born.

God used a plant to teach Jonah,
Of His mercy, and to show his great will
Jonah learned his big lesson
Of God's love and peace be still

You can read all about Jonah, in the book of Jonah.

In the book of Samuel, the 15th chapter, and 22nd verse it says; "*to obey is better than sacrifice.*" God wants His children to have obedient hearts. To be able to listen and learn. I used to read my horoscope (before I was saved) my sign was Taurus the bull. My sign is Jesus now. Anyway the Taurus people were called an stubborn people. What an awful people to be. Stubborn people do not obey. The bible tell us to obey and to respect authority. We have to obey the laws, just like everyone else. To speak evil of no one. *To be peaceful, gentle, showing all humility, to all men.* (Titus 3:1-2). *To obey and respect our parents* (Eph. 6:1-3) and (Col. 3:20). It's time to go back to the old school, and learn respect. Respect for God and His guidance, respect for authority, respect for our parents, and respect for ourselves. You can be respectable in Christ. All you have to do is obey the Word. There it is right back to the word "obey." It's o.k. to, and a must to obey the Father, our creator. He will not lead you astray. Obey Him and live. Let God be your guide.

Now I'd like to talk a little bit about Elijah one of my favorite Prophets. Elijah was a prophet who trusted God and obeyed. Now Elijah had enemies. Idol worshipers, King Ahab and his wife Jezebel. Jezebel was slaughtering the prophets of God. She was looking hard for Elijah, to kill him. He had to run and hide from her.

Run Elijah Run

Run Elijah run, Jezebel is after you
She is slaughtering the
Prophets of God
And she wants to kill you too

God said, go hide in a cave
I'll send the ravens to bring you food
Drink the water from the brook
And stay until I say move

The water in the brook dried up
And now it's time to go
Find the widow in the town
She'll feed you because I said so

I'll stretch the flour and the oil
So you can eat for a long time
Just do as I say do
Because I always take care of mine

God told him to go, and he went. He trusted God, and he obeyed Him. God told him to hide in a cave, near a brook. He sent ravens to feed him, and he drank from the brook. One day the brook went dry, from lack of rain (Elijah had called a drought). God then sent Elijah to Zarephath to a widow, whom God had commanded to provide for him. A step up from the ravens, wouldn't you say? If God said do it, Elijah did it, because he had trust.

Now a little about the widow. The bible never called her by name, but she was a single mother, with a young son. Being a widow, her husband had passed away and she had the responsibilities of raising her son alone. She had to put the food on the table, and it was running out. One day she looked in the flour bin and there was just enough for a small cake, and just enough oil, in her jar to make it. She decided to go gather a couple of sticks to cook her cake, feed her child, and herself one last time, so they could die.

But God was in the plan. Along came Elijah, asking her to give him of her morsel of food, and a drink of water.

The Widow

I'm gathering these few sticks
To cook all that I have left
To feed my child so we can die
And also to feed myself

I will share with you our water
Sure you can have a drink
But the morsel that you ask
Is much harder than you think

The widow said, I have a child
Why should I feed this strange man?
My son and I have so little left
But I must obey his command

Something way down inside me
Down deep within my heart
Tells me to do as he asks
And to obey would be real smart

God touched her heart, and she did as he asked. The flour or the oil did not run dry, just as the Lord had said. Now it didn't end there. In (1 Kings 17:17), the widow woman's son became very ill, so seriously ill, there was no breath in him. If you stop breathing for a long time, you must be dead. Well now, sister widow (since she didn't have a name, I'm calling her sister widow) she let the truth come out. "Why old man of God?" she asked. Is this because of my sin, that you bring it to remembrance? Does my son have to die because of me? She began to remember her sin, one so bad she felt her son's death was a punishment for it. (I don't even want to know). Sometime sin can eat away at us, make us feel guilty, until we take it to the Lord and really let go of it. Even Elijah asked God why?

This is no problem for God. Is this the time to stop trusting God? (I think not). She has done good, Elijah prayed, does she have to lose her son? He prayed for the son's soul to come back, and God sent it back.

This time she was convinced it was God, and only God. I think if I had eaten, fed my child, and a guest, on a morsel of flour and a small amount of oil, for days, I would already been convinced, but she had to see God put breath in her dead son to believe. It's time to stop looking for the big, super, miracles, to believe in the Father, it's time to open our eyes to all the miracles little and big, that He does on a daily basis. We too can feed our children, and the world on God's unchanging Word, and never run out. It's time to trust God and obey.

Chapter 7

In the last chapter, I started to speak of Elijah, the Prophet, and wound up speaking more about the widow, and her son. But Elijah, is so interesting, I'll now try again.

Elijah, asked the people, *"How long will you falter between two opinions? If the Lord is God, follow Him, but if baal follow him* (1 Kings 18:21), *and the people answered not a word.* In the last chapter I talked about how Elijah was running, and hiding, from King Ahab and Queen Jezebel. Well, the Prophet of God, had work to do. He send word to Ahab that he was there, and to meet him.

He asked Ahab to send for the children of Israel, and the four hundred-fifty prophets of baal, to gather on Mount Carmel, for a showdown, him one, them 450, to decide who was truly God.

It reminds me of the old cowboy movies, where the good guy and the bad guy, met at high noon, for the showdown. Well Elijah, was meeting the prophets of baal, to show the people who was the "baddiest" so to speak.

Therefore Elijah, had them, bring two bulls, they could choose one and give him the other. They would cut it into pieces, lay it on wood, and prepare it for sacrifice. Everything but put fire to it. Elijah, would also prepare his bull after that.

Well, the 450 prophets of baal, called him from morning to noon, and no one answered. They cried out, they leaped around, but nothing, I said, nothing happened. Elijah decided to have some fun with them, he knew nothing would happen, so he mocked them saying, "Is he a god?" well, maybe he's asleep, maybe he's busy, or maybe he out of town, on a trip? (our God is never busy, on a trip, or asleep, He is always there when we call Him.) Anyway they cried out, cut themselves, begged, and still nothing happened. Way into the evening sacrifice, nothing, nothing at all.

Then Elijah stepped forward. (In the cowboy movies he would have been wearing the big white hat, and been riding the big white horse). He repaired the altar of God, that was broken down. (always start with a good foundation) he took twelve stones, to represent the number of tribes, and built an altar in the name of the Lord. (you can move mountains if you do it in the name of the Lord). Then he dug a trench around the altar, and poured water over the offering, and the wood, three times, until the water ran over the altar and filled the trench.

Then Elijah prayed, "Dear Lord, let it be known this day, that you are the God, and I am your servant." "Hear me, and show these people, that thou art Lord."

Well, the fire of the Lord fell, and consumed the bull, the wood, the stones, and all the water in the trench. What a mighty God we serve! The people fell on their faces, crying, *"The Lord, He is God!"*

Now this didn't end the adventures of Elijah, to find out more about him, read; (1 Kings 19-2 and 2 Kings 2). I love this guy!

THE SACRIFICE

Elijah said to King Ahab gather
The prophets and the people around
Let me and God show them
Who's the real God in town

You have two hundred-fifty prophets
And I have only me
We can show the people
Just what God wants them to see

Bring two bulls and prepare them
One yours the other mine
Call baal to help you burn him
Now you just take your time

They called, they leaped, they shouted
They even cut their skins
No matter what they did
Their god didn't hear these men

In God's name, Elijah prepared his bull
Soaked it in water in a trench
Soaked it, more and more
Until it just didn't make no sense

But I want you to know
That Elijah had a plan
To show these people
That his God is the man

He called down fire from heaven
And burnt that bull to a crisp
When you put your trust in God
I'll tell you, you can't miss

Chapter 8

Praise the Lord! Don't you love to praise Him? I do! I praise Him because He is so worthy to be praised. My God loves to be worshipped and praised. He is so wonderful. He created us to love us, and how He does love us. Just as you love the child you gave birth to, He loves His creation. He wants to give us everything, and give it more abundantly, (Eph. 3:20).

God's Creation

Behold I stand at the door and knock
Whatever can that mean
That we should open our hearts to God
And we shall be a team

We, of course, are God's creation
Born to a world of sin
Created in His own image
Both women and all men

Our trouble is we don't know God
And all His great powers
We can call on Him and His great love
Call Him at any hour

I believe in God, our Father
Creator of heaven and earth
I know he has been with me
From the moment of my birth

He wants to give us everything, but since the days of Adam, we just have to taste the forbidden fruit. You all know the story of Adam, God's created man? God gave Adam everything. A perfect garden of Eden. Made him lord over the animals. He created him in His own image. (We know how we feel when our own children looks just like us, makes us smile a lot). God gave Adam dominion over every living creature. They all live in harmony, the lion lay with lamb. There was only one command, do not eat from *the tree of knowledge.*

He gave Adam a mate Eve, she was made from Adam's rib, so he wouldn't be lonely. After all that God gave him, he still had to taste the forbidden fruit, with a little urging from his woman, Eve, who listen to the snake.

Adam and Eve

God formed the first man from dust
Adam was his name
Created in the image of God
Over the animals he did reign

He gave him dominion over
The sea, the land, the air
God didn't want him to be alone
So He also put woman there

Although Adam came from earth's dust
Woman came from his side
To live in a garden of Eden
The perfect place to abide

Until one day the serpent
Raised up his ugly head
He caused Eve to tempt Adam
Then their perfect life was dead

Adam was cursed to toil for food
Eve to bare children in pain
Don't listen to that snake children
Deceiving you is his aim

God still loved them. But he had to punish them. We know how that can be, to have to punish our kids, when they are bad. Sometimes, and I said sometimes, it hurts us more than it hurts them. But God's punishment always comes with mercies. God's mercy! Did you know that Moses had his own mercy seat? How about that? A place where he could sit, and receive God's mercy one on one. Just God and him. As the kids say sweet!

God's Mercy Seat
(Ex. 25:22)

My heavenly Father met Moses
Above the mercy seat
Between the cherubim on the ark
From there He did speak

I believe He give us new mercies
And he gives them everyday
Come sit on the seat of mercy
And hear what He has to say

The Lord gives mercy to sinners
And He gives it every time
Just ask and you will receive
His mercy will be thine

To sit on the mercy seat
My sins could wear it out
God forgave me of all those sins
Of that I have no doubt

Sinners won't you come and sit
This seat is for you too
Come and receive His mercy
It is there for you and you

Now, I ask you, what is mercy? We ask the Lord for it, all the time, "Lord, have mercy on me," but what is it and why do we want it?

The dictionary, says;

- Show of pity or leniency (of mild and tolerant disposition or effect).
- Divine blessing

Most of the time we are asking the Lord to show us pity, or special favor, to ease our broken hearts, or to have mercy in our finances. We ask Him for special blessing too. We ask for mercy all the time. Now do we have to be special like Moses to receive His blessings? NO!

- (Ex. 20:60) tells us thousands can get it
- (Num.14:18) tells us we don't have to fight for it; He has it in abundant.
- (1Chron. 16:34) tells us to give thanks for God is good; and His mercies endureth for ever.
- (Ps. 100:5) tells us not only is He good, His mercy is everlasting.

Even though His mercies last for ever, He gives us new mercies everyday. He gave mercy over a death sentence in (2 Kings 20:1-6).

God tells us in (Hosea 6:6), and (Matt. 9:3), He's not interested in fake hearts and prayer, sacrifices, that mean nothing, He want us to show Him we have mercy in our hearts. Then we can show true love and worship of Him. We can show mercy to our fellowman. We have to be like Jesus, (Eph. 2:4) tells us, God is rich in mercy. It took His great love, and grace to save us, and His mercy keeps us daily (Titus 3:5). Not by our good works we have done, but according to His mercy, He saved us. He gives us a renewing of the Holy Spirit, which He gave us through our Savior, Jesus Christ. He sent his only Begotten Son, to earth in human form. Jesus had a human family, mother, father, brothers, and sisters. He had friends that He loved. There is one friend I would like to talk about right now. In (John 11:35) it says two words; *Jesus wept.* This known to be the shortest verse in the bible. One of the first verses memorized by children, because it is so short. Jesus wept! Jesus cried! His human form wept for his friend, Lazarus, was dead.

Jesus Wept.

Jesus wept, the shortest verse
But it's message is so strong
His friend Lazarus passed away
Why? Did Jesus take to long?

No, He waited, a miracle to perform
To show the world His mighty grace
But never to do harm

He walked the waters
He calmed the angry seas
He turned a raging storm
Into a gentle sea breeze

Yet He wept

Let's think about this for a moment. Jesus is the son of God. Performing miracles was one of the many things he did, here on Earth. In fact, let's go back a few days.

Lazarus was sick, very, very sick. His sisters, Mary and Martha, (Mary was the one who anointed his feet with fragrant oil, and wiped them with her hair). These were good friends of Jesus. Therefore, when Lazarus got sick, they sent for the one whom they knew could make him well again, Jesus!

When Jesus received word, he stayed two more days, where He was. Then He said to His disciples, "Let's go back to Judea." his disciples didn't want Him to go back, for the Jews had wanted to stone Him there. In other words, throw rocks at him until they killed Him. But of course Jesus was the one, who gave up His life, he chose the time and the place, and it was not His time yet. So He avoided them.

Jesus told them Lazarus was dead. I am glad, for your sakes, so you will believe, He said, so back they went.

As soon as Martha heard Jesus, was coming, she ran to meet Him, saying, "I know, Lord, if you had been here our brother would not have died." Jesus replied, "Your brother will rise again, this day, if you believe in me." Martha said, "I believe." Then Mary also came to where he was, she was weeping. Jesus was troubled and groaned in the spirit. *Jesus wept.*

Although, he was there to raise Lazarus up, he was still pained by Mary and Martha's pain, and he cried with them. It wasn't the only time Jesus wept, he wept for Jerusalem. (Luke 19:41). I'm sure he still cry for the lost souls, that refuse to turn their lives around, and die in sin. Don't make Him cry for you.

They went to the grave, where Lazarus lay dead four days, and was beginning to smell. And that smell is no joke. We lost a cousin, in Texas heat, and it was several days before she was discovered. That's a smell, I'll never forget. It didn't bother Jesus. First he thanked God, His father, then calling loudly, he said, "Lazarus, come forth," Lazarus came out with his grave clothes still wrapped around him. "Loose him," said Jesus, "Let him go," and they did.

Loose Him

Your brother will rise again
Although dead and in his grave
To show my father's awesome power
I will raise him from where he lays

But, Lord, he is rotting by now
I'm sure he's smelling bad
That's why we are gathered here
And why we are so sad

Martha, Mary, and their friends
For Lazarus they all cried
Jesus also wept with them
For His good friend had died

They went to the cave that was
His grave, and took away the stone
Jesus prayed, then yelled "come forth"
He emerged with grave clothes on

Loose him now, and let him go
Is what Jesus had to say
All the people who gathered there
Saw a miracle that same day

Now we are heirs, and the hope for eternal life. We can show others
the mercy that God has given us. If you are bound, let Jesus loose you.
He is still in the business of setting the captives free. He will free you.

Chapter 9

You've Got To Love It, To Live It

I gave my life to Christ one day
I got tired of a sinful world
I gave up my worldly lusts
Decided to give Him a whirl

I cried out for him to save me
And gave up drinking, smoking, and such
So if I hold on to these "little sin"
Maybe no one will notice them much

Then I began to study, to live
And know what God's Word said
To live this life, you have to love it
Is what I though I read

I know that I love Christ
And I love the life I live
No sin, I know big or small
Is worth living without His

You have to love it in order to live it
I know this is true
I live this life because I love it
It's what I want to do

Many people find it hard to live a saved life. Why? Because they love the things of the world, more, than they love God. One thing that I find is, if you love the life you live, it makes it easier. In fact I'll go so far as to say, you've got to love it to live it. First of all, I love God! I love me some God! He's my rock, He's my shield, He's my mother and my father, He means everything to me. I can call Him when I'm happy, I can call Him, when I'm sad. He's by my side when I wake up in the morning, and He's there when I go to bed each night. He never leaves me, because He loves me. I may try to leave Him, but He never leaves me. The only way you can walk away from that kind of love is to love something else more. If it's hard to stay saved, it's because you love sin more than God. That's right, you love that sin, that you can't give up more, than you love God.

And even more important than my loving Him, is knowing that He loves me. The most quoted verse in the Bible is (John 3:16) it tells us *"God so loved the world, that He gave his only begotten son; that whosoever, believeth on him will not perish...* he gave his son for me. Now that's love. It makes me want to praise Him, I love to praise Him, night and day. I love to read the word, I love to live the word, I love to hear the word, I love to speak the word, I love to sing the word, I don't live this life because I fear hell, although that a good reason, I would rather have a mansion in heaven, rather than to burn in hell's fire. I love this life, that's reason enough for me.

You see I love to greet people in Jesus' name. I love to walk in the blood of the lamb, so others may see God in me.I love to read the poems God gave me, and I love to sing His praises, (even my voice sound good to Him), ilove to dance and shout. I love to wake up in the morning with sweet dreams of Him.

WHEN GOD WAKES YOU

Has God ever woke you in the middle of the night
And told it's time to pray?
He'll tell you to get on your knees
And can keep you sometimes til daybreaks
Sometimes His message is short and sweet
Sometimes it takes awhile
Sometimes it'll make you cry
Sometimes it will make you smile

When you're saved and sanctified
And God talks to you
You know you are his child
And God cares what you do

Sometimes He has a warning
So you'd better take heed
Sometimes He answers right then and there
And gives you what you need

When God calls you in the midnight
Hours tell you to pray
Get up, get on your knees
Listen to what he has to say

I just love the life I live, sometimes I have trials and they can be hard, but I have God to call on, that makes them easier. There are some things in this Christian life that I find to be hard to do. Don't get me wrong, loving God is easy, there was a time I found it hard to get up and speak in front of people, now I even love that. I love it, because God gives me such wonderful things to say about Him. Then what do you ask, do I find hard to do? Well, I'm trying to eliminate gossip from my lips, and my ears. Don't come to me with I heard, O.K.? It's hard for me to trust God for my finances, I still live from paycheck to paycheck, and when something comes up unexpectedly, the first thing to go is my tithes. Wrong move! I am trusting God much more in that area now. I find it hard to keep my mind saved. My mind can go places you would not believe. That's why I would rather read a book, then one that has been made into a movie, your imagination will take you where the actors can't. Why is it so hard for me, because I'm trying to do it, and not letting the Holy Spirit lead me. It doesn't have to be hard, if I would just stop making it hard.

I love the way he heals the sick through my prayers, I love the way he renews my salvation, I love the way He loves me, even though I'm not perfect. Yes it's true I'm not perfect, but He loves me anyway. Now you see why I love this life? I receive rewards everyday, new mercies, new salvation, new life, new grace, new love, and a renewing of the Holy Spirit. If you got it, you got to love it, therefore, you got to love it, to live it. You have to love it more than you love that sin you're holding on too. More than you love cigarettes, alcohol, gambling and crack, more than you love lying, fighting, or backbiting, more than you love cussing, fornicating, or gossiping.

Love of the Word, will mean more to you than any sin, you can do. You have to love this life to live it, praise the Lord I love it.

HOSANNA

We shall love the Lord with all
Our heart and with all our soul
With all thy mind, and all thy strength
This is the first commandment told

Then love thy neighbor as thy self
There's no commandment greater then these
There is one God and one God only
There is none other greater than He

To have this true love in your heart
It is greater than sacrifice
Give Him love with all your strength
Our Lord Jesus gave this advice

Do not err, because you know not
The scriptures, nor do you know God's power
Blessed savior, that He cometh
And we know not the hour

Hosanna, blessed be the Father
Bless be His Holy name
Since I found you, my loving Savior
I will never be the same

Chapter 10

THE HARVEST

The harvest is plentiful
But the labors are few
Pray to the Lord to
Send laborer unto you

When sheep lose their shepherd
They scatter aboard
Come, work for Jesus
And never get tired

Go ye and preach
The kingdom is at hand
Heal the sick, raise the dead
You work for the man

Provide neither gold or silver
Nor brass in your purse
Your pay comes from Heaven
And not from this Earth

Work, work, for Jesus
Get some dust on your feet
Work, work, for Jesus
With every word you speak
(Matt. 9-10)

I remember some years ago. There was this company. I know they sold soap, I can't remember what else they sold, but I remember the soap. They would get you to be an investor, and once you were aboard, you would constantly talk about their produce to others, trying to get them to invest. Everywhere you went, and everyone you saw, you would talk the produce, tying to sell and get others to come aboard, to sell it. They talked about it in the grocery store, at socials, at work, and everywhere they went, until they had people either buying it, or hiding when they saw them coming.

Well, that's the way we should be about Jesus. We should be talking about, and telling of Him, trying to get others to join Him, so they can also tell others about Him.

The soap company was all about making money, the more people they had selling, the more money they made. We should be winning soul to Christ like that. The more sinners we get to give their hearts to God, the more God, gives the increase. Then that new saved person will tell someone about Jesus and so on and so forth. We indeed must do God's work.

DO GOD'S WORK

We are all of one body
God needs us one and all
Each part works with the other
To make us stand tall

Without eyes we cannot see
And ears we cannot hear
A foot, a hand, a toe
Each part we hold dear

The church needs a whole body
If it's going to work
Deacons, teachers, poets, and preachers
All make up our church

I don't want to hear
"I can't do this" or "I can't do that"
Do what God gave you to do
Or He may take it back

The more we sow the more we reap. Listen, not only must you sow, you must sow good seed, and watch out for the sower of tares. (an undesirable weed). For they are wicked. (Matt. 13:37-38). Only God can give the increase. *So then neither he who plants is anything; nor he who waters, but God who gives the increase.* (1 Cor. 3:7) The 8th verse tells us, *he who waters, and he who plants are one, and each will receive his own reward, according to his own labor.*

So we must be like the soap salesman, we must tell of Jesus everywhere we go. We must live like Jesus in whatever we do. We must sow his seed, and win souls to Christ, then God will give the increase.

Chapter 11

In this chapter, I will talking about the fruit of the Spirit, found in (Gal. 5:22). *The fruit of the Spirit: love, joy, peace, kindness, goodness, faithfulness, gentleness, self-control, and long-suffering, against such there is no law.*

They are called the fruit of the Spirit, not fruits, because they are one, *love*! It always starts with love. That's always the best place to start. After love it can only get better. Joy, peace, long-suffering. Wait! How did that get in there? Do we have to suffer a long time, right in the middle of love, joy and kindness? What does long-suffering mean, and how did it get in the middle of the fruit of the Spirit?

The dictionary says it mean; bearing trouble, ect, patiently for a long time. (sounds like Jesus to me).

O.K. bearing our troubles, patiently, for a long time. I would say, there is where self-control, and peace comes in. all the fruit work together, to keep us saved. How easy it would be to sin, if the fruit was not in us.

Can you commit adultery, or fornication, with the friut inside you? I think not. For you have faithfulness, and self-control to keep you from that. How about idolatry, envy, murderous thoughts, or jealousies? They can't exist in the same heart as love, joy, faithfulness, goodness, kindness, gentleness, peace, yes, and long-suffering, which is patience and self-control.

The flesh lusts for the things of the world, as Christians we walk in the Spirit. The Holy Spirit's fruit is to be manifested in our lives every bit as much as His gifts are to be shown through us. With His fruit in us, we don't hang out with the old gang. We come away from worldly things. With His fruit in us, we don't have little flings. We only have sex with out our married spouses (married to us of course). With His fruit in us, we don't envy you, your new car or new house.

We wait patiently (Longsuffering) on the Lord, for our blessings. They will come, we have God's word on it. God loves us

All you need is love. (Gal. 5:14). The whole law of God can be summed up in one word, that word of course is *love*. The act of love covers so much. When you love your are happy, (Joy). When you love, you are full of (peace),when you love you are patient, (Long-suffering), when you love you show (kindness) and (goodness). When you love you are (faithful) when you love you are (Gentle) and have (self- control), slow to anger, against such there is no law. We who are Christ's have crucified the flesh, we walk in the Spirit. We live in the Spirit. (Gal. 5:24-25).

Kill that sinful flesh, walk in the Spirit, you'll find it to be delicious. Mmm, mmm, that's good. Try it you'll like it.

The Fruit

We who are Christians
Have crucified the flesh
We walk in the Spirit
And are continually blessed

The fruit of the Spirit
Starts out with love
The fruit that God gave us
He sends it from above

Joy, peace, long suffering,
Are just to name a few
Kindness, goodness, gentleness
Are there for us to use

Without the fruit inside us
Sin would run amuck
Without the fruit inside me
My life would be yuck

To have the fruit inside me
Means I've given up all sin
They manifest within us
So we can show all men

They all work together
They always start with love
All working together
To make us gentle as a dove

Chapter 12

Dear Jesus

Dear Jesus,
I love you, I love you with all my heart
And I will never let satan tear us apart
You've already proved how much you love me
By dying on the cross, dear Lord, you open
My eyes to see
Your Father, who is my Father now
Gave you to me, with lots of love just to show me how
Your love is so innocent, so sweet, and so pure
You left for me, to show your love, the blessed
Comforter
I'd like to take this time, to thank you once again
You see, I'd like to share your love
With all those in sin
Now it's time to bring this letter to an end
But not my love which grows stronger
As I share you with all men
I love you, Lord

Yours forever
Your child

When it comes to talking about Jesus, there is so much to say. I have so many poems about Him. He is a wonderful Savior. From the time He was sent to Earth, (*the Word became flesh*), (John 1:14) His life has been a blessing.

He was a blessing to Mary, His mother, He was conceived by the Holy Ghost, to a young lady, who had not known man. A virgin, something most young girls today, don't want to be anymore. You know, being virtuous, when they marry? Thanks to the lifestyles of today, sex is very readly done, at a very young age. Ready or not.

Jesus was a blessing to Joesph, who was betrothed to Mary, married her and did not know her until after Jesus was born. They then had several children of their own.

Jesus, knew he had a job to do for His Heavenly Father, He went forth in His name, preaching the gospel.

After being water baptized by John, (known as John the Baptist, He was a blessing to him also), the Heavens opened up, the Spirit of God decended down to Him in the form of a dove. God spoke and said, *"This is my beloved son, in whom I am well pleased."* (Matt. 3:17).

Jesus was then led, by the Spirit, up into the wilderness to be tempted by the devil. The devil , he is something else, indeed he is, or so he thinks. I know he's going to and fro in the land seeking whom he may devour. Thinking he has rule over us, but the only power he has, is what we give him. Jesus didn't give him any, and you know he couldn't tempt Him. (Matt. 4:1-11). We, just like Jesus, can overcome satan by standing strong, in the Word of God. I don't know what makes the devil think, that what he has to offer, is as appealing, as what God is giving us. Maybe the weak-minded thinks it is. He can only offer you a eternity of fire and brimstone.

Jesus came to offer us life-everlasting. With me there is no contest, I'll take Jesus every time.

Jesus went through the land, teaching, healing, raising the dead, and casting out demons.

JESUS THE TEACHER

I say to you, "Arise take up your bed and walk"
He then went to the seaside, where He again taught
He passed the son of Alphae, and said "follow Me"
Those who complained, He open their eyes to see

The Pharisees tried to give satan God's due
"How can you cast out devils, unless they be in you?"
Jesus answered saying, "How can satan cast out satan?
A divided house can't stand
If satan rise up against himself
He will surely end

All sins shall be forgiven, unto the son of man
But blaspheme against the Holy Ghost
And you could be eternally damned
(Mark 2:11-14) (Mark 3:22-29)

And now, Jesus the healer:

BORN BLIND

The Jews didn't believe concerning Him
The blind could see but their sights were dim
A man called Jesus made the clay
That opened his eyes to see that day

They called his parents to prove them right
His parents said "No" he was born with no sight
These words were spoken for they feared the Jews
He is of age let him answer you

Be he sinner I know not
But he gave me sight right on the spot
Now you ask what he did for me
Where I was blind I now can see

He also raised the dead,

SHE'S NOT DEAD

Why make ye this ado and weep
The girls not dead, but asleep
He put them out who laughed to scorn
And took the parents, who did mourn

Little girl I say to you arise
She sat up and opened her eyes
This girl of twelve rose to her feet
At his command she was given to eat

He spoke in parables, so we could understand;
PARABLES

Jesus explained things by parables
So we could understand
He used the birds, candles, and seeds
To enlighten man

If you put your candle under a
Basket where no one can see
You'll be doing no good for anyone
You won't be helping me

For there is nothing hidden
That will not come to light
Don't think you can get away
Because it's done at night

When the sower sows his seeds
Take heed to where they go
If they land on bad ground
They may never grow

But when they fall on good ground
They yield a healthy crop
That yield and yield and yield, and yield
Good seed you cannot stop

He cast out demons, and at one time, caused hundreds of them to enter into swine, and caused the swine to destroy themselves, (Mark 5:1-20).

Isn't that what is happening, right now today? The demon are causing many people to destroy themselves. You don't have to let the devil destroy you. Jesus can set you free. He loves you, so love yourself and accept His love. He will set you free.

Chapter 13

Have you ever been to a concert on the grass? Where you go to see an artist, at a outside stadium, and you sit on the grass? As long as the artist gave what you came to hear, you stayed and enjoyed it. Of course you brought "stuff" with you to be comfortable, inside and out.

Well, Jesus, and His disciples emerged from the boat in a deserted place. A great multitude, had gathered, to hear Him speak. You could say, Jesus held the first concet on the grass. (Mark 6:39).

When the hour was growing late, his disciples, came to Him saying, "The hour is late, send them home so they can eat, for they have no food." now this is where Jesus' concert differs from yours. He had the disciples gather what was there in way of food. It turned out to be, five loaves and a few fish. (in today's concert those who had money could eat, those without, well sorry).

Jesus took the few loaves and fish, and looked up to Heaven. Blessed the food, and fed at least five thousand, to their fill, and had some left over. (Matt.6:30-44). Now that's a concert. Better than the fireworks, on fourth of July! And even better, the Word, is free. Paid for later on, by the blood of Christ our Savior.

TEACHER
(Luke 9)

From five loaves and a few fish
Jesus fed the multitude
Over five thousand ate to fill
That's what He can do

He healed the sick, raised the dead
And calmed the angry sea
He said, to all pick up your cross
Come and follow me

Anyone who follows me
Must give me all your needs
Pick up your cross, and everyday
Stay close to me indeed

Whosoever loses his life for my sake
Will be saving it instead
If you choose, the world and fame
You might as well be dead

A man said teacher help my son
He has a demon thru and thru
I begged your disciples, they couldn't help
Now I'm asking you

O stubborn faithless people
How long must I put up with you
He cast the demon from the boy
And showed us what faith can do

Chapter 14

Wouldn't it be wonderful, if we could go into the bathroom, fill the sink with water, lather your hands with soap, and wash all your sins away? Some us would need a pretty large bar of soap. Think of how easy it would be to wash away hate, unforgiveness, or envy. To wash away lying, gossiping, and backbiting. To wash away the blood that Jesus shed for us on the cross.

Pilate tried! He thought a little water in a basin, could make him feel less guilty, about setting a murderer free, rather than Jesus, who had done nothing to deserve this. (Matt. 27:24)

To give Pilate his due, he tried to free Jesus, but the people cried out, "give us Barabbas, crucify Jesus. It was Jesus' time.

CRUCIFY HIM

What should I do with him
This so called King of the Jews
Pilate asked the people
I leave it all up to you

"Crucify him", "crucify him"
Is what the crowd of people said
We want you to crucify him
We want to see him dead

Pilate then released Barabbas
He had to let someone go
They took our Lord to die
The choose our Savior, don't you know

So Pilate, washed his hands
As if it would make him clean
He blamed the crowd, to place the guilt
Well, so it would seem

Jesus was the King back then
And He's the King of all now
I cant' wait to see His holy face
At His feet I will bow

It was indeed the will of God, that Jesus, his only begotten son, die for our sins. The prophecy was fulfilled.

Maybe if we could wash away the pain, that Jesus, suffered, it would ease our minds, the cross that He bore would seem a little lighter. A little soap and water, would wash away the blood, from the wound in His side, and ease the pain from the thorne crown, he wore on His head. Wash away the agony, that the angels, who attended Him on Earth, must have felt, when they couldn't reach out to help Him, as He suffered.

Well, soap and water, can't wash away our sins, but the blood of Jesus, washed them away. We can't wash away His blood, but the blood has washed away our sins. For us He suffered and died. But the grave couldn't hold Him, he arose.

HE AROSE

An angel sent the women, not one but a few
To tell the disciples, what they already knew
He had a risen, rose up from the grave
The grave where thee days ago, He was laid
He arose
To die on the cross that day, was His plan
To be buried, rise again, and ascend for this land
He arose

His disciples ran to the tomb, for a peep
Found he had arisen, now that's pretty deep
He appeared before others, on that faithful day
Now we have the message,
He has shown us the way

He arose, he has risen
Now He is home

The angels couldn't help Him down off the cross, but an angel came down from heaven, in a earthquake, and rolled the stone away. (Matt. 28:2). Jesus went home!

What a homecoming that must have been. All Heaven must have been rejoicing. What a party they must have had.

Although, He went home, He is still with us, (Matt.28:16-20), tells us, He is with us until the end of the Earth. Therefore, I'm working here on Earth, so I can have a home with Him, when I die. I don't need soap and water, all I need is His word. He said to preach, the Kingdom of Heaven is at hand. I believe Him, and I'm on my way to heaven, won't you come with me?

I'M ON MY WAY TO HEAVEN

I am here on Earth preaching
The Kingdom of heaven is at hand
It's time to turn your life around
Can you hear me sinner man?

I'm looking forward to
A new life of no more sin
When I die here on Earth
my life will just begin

I'm on my way to heaven
Won't you come with me?
I want to be with Jesus
And there's so much to see

The streets are paved with gold
And there's a pearly gate
I'll have my own mansion there
When I reach that perfect place

One day when Jesus died for me
He gave his life upon the cross
I got the message He sent to me
So my soul will not be lost

He died for you too, won't you come along? Get on board the glory
train, it will take you home.

Chapter 15

Can you stand the test?

It's easy to say we trust God in all things, and we really mean it when we say it. But when the trials come up, and oh, they are coming, can we stand the test?

We know the story of Job? (Job 1:6-8), Job was a blameless, upright man, who feared God, and shunned evil. He did nothing wrong to be punished for.

So many imes when trials come on us, we ask, "Lord, what did I do wrong?" "I don't deserve this." remember the widow lady's son? Her first question was, "Was this a sin, that I have done?"

Well, Job, this man of wealth, and possessions, loved and worshipped God. He had seven sons, and three daughters. (You know having sons was a special thing in those days, sons and female donkeys). He really had it going on. Job served the Lord in all things, and saw to it his family did too. Satan, not God, caused him to lose everything. God let satan go ahead and try Job, because satan though he could cause Job to turn on God.

Job lost cattle, wealth, servants, and all his precious children. Job was beside himself, he tore his robe, and shaved his head, but said he, *"Naked I came, and naked I shall return, the Lord giveth, and the Lord taketh away, blessed be the name of the Lord.* (Job 1: 20).

Old Satan wasn't through yet, nope, he attacked Job's health. Job's trust was with God. One thing about trust, you *know* that when you trust God, he will never let you down, no matter how things looks to everyone else. (in fact, you could say having trust is having a surgeon, by the name of Butcher. I did and he was a very good doctor).

Anyway, Job's wife, (she was still there, she to could have been taken), lost all of her integrity, (those were her children and wealth too), she saw how her man was suffering, she just gave up. She told Job, "You should curse your God and die." But trust told Job, this was not God, who did this, and even if He had, He must have had a reason. Can we stand the test?

His friends gave up, his wife gave up, and Job cursed the day of his birth, (Job 3:1), but his trust in God remained strong. Now, he got despondent, (Job 13:20), but Job did not fail the test. He wavered, and brought forth the voice of God, in a whirlwind, (Job 38:1; 40:1-2). When God spoke to Job, (Job 40:3-4), Job said "shut my mouth." You see our trouble is we don't listen to God, when He speaks to us. He speaks to us ,we just don't hear. Job listened and obeyed.

Well, Job stood the test, and was totally restored. His wealth, his servants, his cattle, he even had seven sons, and three daughters again. (I'm sure he had a few female donkeys too).

Because he served God from a pure heart, with real love, and genuine trust, all was doubled unto him. (Job 16:33). So Job died and was old and full of days. He stood the test, can you?

JOB

Job was a man of God, who was
Blessed with cattle, and lots of wealth
He had seven sons, three daughters
He also was blessed with good health

Satan saw this man of God and
Thought he could make him sin
He made a deal with God
One he thought he could win

God said he could try Job
As long as he was kept alive
Go ahead do your worst
Job will stay on God's side

Job lost cattle, servants, and children
He tore his clothes and shaved his head

The devil thought he had him
But he praised God instead

The the devil gave Job sores
And boils, that had pus and lots of pain
His wife said "curse your God and die"
Can't you see He's the blame

But Job stay strong in God
He knew God would not do that
Because of his strong trust
God gave him his wealth back

He gave him back his servants
And gave him children too
Put your trust in God, my friend
And see what He'll do for you

This is a quiz, I tried in my church one time. It is for saved people who should take a look at their Christian lives. We did!

How days a <u>month</u>:

- Do you go to work? Be on time?
- Do you go to church? Be on time?
- Do you go to the beauty, or barber shop? Be on time?
- Get your nails and toes done?
- Go shopping (food or otherwise)?
- Pay tithes?
- <u>Study</u> your Bible?
- Put on make-up?
- Play golf?
- Go to Bible study or prayer meeting?
- Pray in secret?
- Brush your teeth?
- Bathe?
- Dedicate time to church functions?
- How often do you pray for your Pastor?
- How often do you pray for your church?
- How often do you fast and for how long?
- Do you have a prayer closet? Do you use it?

I know some of these questions sound silly, of course, you bathe and brush your teeth every day. (We hope). And your work week is usually five days. Well, what about the time we give to God is it automatic as well? Do we pay tithes regularly, just as we buy food? After church on Sunday, do our Bible go back on the shelve, until next Sunday? How much time do we give God? Give fasting, and praying? How about worship? It's time to make God part of our everyday lives.

How can we? You say, when our lives are so busy? Well now, you could pray and worship in the shower. Use your break time at work to read and memorize, a bible verse. In fact read your bible instead of a magazine, when you are under the dryer at the beauty shop. Biblical tapes, and gospel CD's in traffic can soothe you. They help you to relax, and replace some road rage. Plan some time each day for your secret closet, and go one on one with the Father.

Jesus called his discipiles to be fishers of men, we too are His disciples, go fishing. The sinners are biting. In order for us to do this, we must be strong in the Word. We can get strong by attending bible study regularly, prayer meetings, reading our bibles, and using our secret closets.

There it is again, secret closet, some of you don't know what that is, right? Some of you younger saints are probably asking why do I need one? Isn't that something they used to do, in the olden days? I go to the altar, on Sunday, and even prayer meeting sometimes, why do I need a secret closet at home? Well, Jesus, said, *we should pray, not to be seen by man, but in a secret place, with your door shut, with just you and the Father. Pray in secret and He will reward you openly.* (Matt. 6:5-6).

When you shut yourself away, in a quiet place, you can hear God, when He speaks to you. We just have to learn to wait on Him. Now a days, there is a time limit on prayer time. I remember in the "olden days" there were shut-in's at church. Members would bring their children, dressed in pajamas, with blankets and pillows, made them pallets, while they lingered on the altar all night. Praying and waiting on the Lord. And we had alters in those days, where you could bow down, on your knees, and pray. Many new churches don't have altars, any more. God should be bowed down too, and praised. (Phil. 2:10-11), tells us every knee shall bow, and every tongue confess, that Jesus Christ is Lord.

So enter your secret place, bow down to Him, and give Him some praise. Worship Him! Just praise Him for all His glory, for all He has done for you, without asking Him for something in return. He already knows what you need, so just thank Him, and worship Him. He is real! You're going to have a real good time.

MY SECRET PLACE

I have a place I love to go
I call it my secret place
Where I can get down on my knees
And enter into God's grace

It is very quite there
Where I can be one on one with Him
With Jesus, and the Holy Ghost
I can speak to the three of them

I love to give Him all my praise
For He loves me without a doubt
Sometimes I spend some quite time
And sometimes I have to shout

In my secret closet
I don't go there for show
What I say to my Father there
Is for only us to know

Chapter 17

Let's talk about some of the biblical women, that had contact, with Jesus, our Savior. Maybe even some from the old testament, we'll see how God leads me. The first is the woman with an issue of blood.

I can imagine what it was like for the woman, *twelve years,* she bled. she went from doctor to doctor, she suffered many cures, that did not work. (Mark 5:26), until she was broke. They were no help to her at all. They just couldn't stop the flow, it only grew worse. (Today they would give her a hysterectomy, and send her home). Of course, we too can be healed by faith, if we believe.

Anyway, this woman, heard about a man, a man called Jesus, a man who healed the sick, and raised the dead. She must have thought, if only I could get to him, I know I would be healed. But there was a big crowd around Him, when she got there. I, imagine, she was weak, from the years of flowing, no doubt an anemic as well. Blood lost can mean, iron loss, so in her weaken state, she couldn't push through the crowd, and may have ended up crawling, and could only reach, His hem.

The minute, she touched Him, her flow dried up, and she was healed. (Mark 5:29).

Jesus immediately, felt the power go from him, and asked, "Who has touched my clothes? With such a crowd around Him, his disciples, answered, "It could be anyone, how can you tell?" as Jesus looked around for the person, the woman, shaking with fear, answered, "It was I ."

Then she told Him the whole truth. Jesus said to her, "Daughter, thy faith has healed you, go in peace, and be whole.

Now put yourself in her place, for the first time in twelve years, the flow was gone, the smell was gone, (blood has an odor) , the weakness was gone, all dried up, with faith and a touch, she was made whole. I'm sure as she walked home, there was a bounce in her steps. People must have said, "She went from sick to crazy," I know I would have shouted all the way home.

THE HEM OF HIS GARMENT

I've seen so many doctors
Over the last twelve years
Paid out all my money and
To this day I'm still not healed

I'm so tired of bleeding
Now what else can I do
"I'm sorry" they all told me
We just can't heal you

But on day I heard
Of a healing man
A man they call Jesus
Now I believe He can

The crowd that surrounds Him
Is big and I'm so weak
I'll get down on my knees
And try to touch His feet

If I can just touch His garment
There I've touched His hem
I know that faith has healed me
I can feel it in my limbs

Who has touched me?
I heard the Savior say
Although I was shaking
I spoke up and said, "hey"

> Jesus with loving kindness
> Said, "By your faith you are healed"
> Thank-you loving Father
> I will always do your will

Let us not forget that faith is still working miracles today. Your faith can make you whole.

Then there was the woman from Samarita, that Jesus met at the well. He was tired and his disciples, went into town to get food, while He rested by the well. This woman came to the well to get water. Jesus asked for a drink. She answered I am Samaritan, you are a Jew, why are you asking me sir, since Jews have no dealing with us? Jesus said, "If only you knew, who you were talking too, and what I can give you." I can give you living water.

Well, said the woman, this is a very deep well, and you have nothing to draw with, where can you get this living water? Jesus replied, "*With this water you will thirst again, whosoever drinks of the living water, will never thirst again. You will have a fountain of water, springing up into everlasting life.*

Now let us reflect on this a moment. I live in a town where we get some very hot weather. We just had seventeen straight days of over 100 degrees. I drink lot of ice cold water, and as cold as it is when I drank it, I soon get thirsty and have to drink again. Over and over, again. But right after I drink I am so refreshed, I just feel good all over. That's the way I feel, since I drank from the fountain of living water, that Jesus offered. I am refreshed and it stays with me, and it will last forever. It doesn't go away on Monday, and stay away until Sunday morning, that's not it. The water that Jesus is offering, is the fountain of the everlasting water of life. (John 4:14).

Jesus offered her the chance to experience, a new life. One that came with life everlasting, the Holy Spirit, and the chance to worship in spirit and in truth. Jesus than told her to run and get her husband, and bring him here. She answered, "Husband, I have no husband." Jesus said, "This is true, you have had five husbands, but the one you have now is not married to you." Well she marveled at this and ran to tell everyone, that she had met a man, who told her, all that she had done. She became a true believer, she had met Christ.

AT THE WELL

Jesus met a Samaritan woman
And asked her for a drink
You Jews don't deal with us
Now what do you think?

Jesus said, I can give you water
And you'll never thirst again
I can give you living water
If you give up your sin

Now go get your husband
And bring him back here
Oh, I have no husband
She said with a swear

Jesus answered saying
"I'm sure this is true
You have had five husbands
But this one did not marry you

She ran into town, yelling
He's told me what I've done
He must be Christ, I'm telling you
I'm sure he's the one

There also was the woman Jesus met on the Sabbath. Little is said about her, but it was powerful. She had a spirit of infirmity, (physical weakness,or defect), for eighteen years. It had her bent over, and she couldn't straighten up. (Luke 13:10-17).

Jesus laid hands on her and said, *"Woman thou art loose, from thy infirmity,"* and she was immediately made straight. She then glorified God.

THOU ART LOOSED

Jesus healed a woman who
Was bent over for eighteen years
She could not straighten up
I'm sure this caused her some tears

Although it was the Sabbath
Jesus said, "Woman thou art loosed
She immediately was straighten
And she knew this was no ruse

She began to glorifiy the Father
And give Him the highest praise
It probably caused among them
A brow or two to raise

Then Jesus had to straighten
Out these hypocrites
He is our Lord and Savior
Only God knows what's best

It don't take much, it can happen just like that with you. All the sins that have you bound, so you can't straighten up, can be loosed. Give them up, glorify God. He's waiting.

Now here they come again, those hypocrites, that criticize. They could not appreciate the miracle of the woman being healed, because it was done on what they thought was the wrong day. Jesus had to teach them there is no wrong day for healing. Do we have to suffer, pain, sin and woes, because, there is only one day we can pray? Or only one person that can pray for us? I think not. It's time to put your adversaries to shame, and loose the bounds of satan. Jesus will straighten you up, His office is open everyday, all day and all night. Call Him, He's in!

Remember the woman who was caught in adultery, and was brought to Jesus for condemnation? What did Jesus say to the crowd, that brought her? *He who is without sin, let him cast the first stone.* (John 8:4-11) Remember this also, you can't remove a splinter from your brother's eye, when you have a beam in your own (Matt. 7:3). First let us clean up our own acts, then we can show others the way to Jesus. Don't tell them, show them, by doing. Then we will rejoice at the one that is found.

THE FOUND

Rejoice and be glad for the
One sheep that is found
Not the ninety-nine that are safe
For they are still around

The ninety-nine good sheep
Will have their rewards too
But the lost that is found
God will rejoices over you

When you have ten coins
And one falls from your hand
You look until you find it
Like God does for man

You see God loves us
The good and the bad
He doesn't want to lose
Not one lass or lad

Repent and be welcome
Back into the fold
You are never to young
For Jesus, or you're never to old

Remember the wages of sin is death, but the gift of God is eternal life.

THE WAGES OF SIN

Have you been set free from sin
And became one of God's servants?
Letting go of a sinful life
Not caring which way sin went?

For the wages of sin is death
But the gift of God is eternal life
Walking in His grace and righteousness
Knowing this walk is right

Live not like a dead man
Thinking I've got time
If this is the way your thinking
Your sinful life ain't worth a dime

Please, don't let sin rule you
When you can be a slave to righteousness
Living under God's truth and grace
And knowing His way is best

Be a slave to righteousness, walk in truth and grace. God will bless you, and remember this, God loves you, and so do I.

Chapter 18

What kind of witness am I?

My new King James version bible, explains witnessing as, giving evidence, attesting, confirming, confessing, bearing record, speaking well of, giving a good report, testifying that one has seen, heard, or experienced.

The word witnessing is what Paul, used to describe himself, to the King (Acts 26:22), and indeed he was. He went from being a persecutor of Christians, to being persecuted. It then became part of he testimony.

When Stephen was stoned, (a different meaning than being stoned today), they threw rocks at him until he was dead. Paul, known then as Saul, was there, consenting to his death. He even guarded the clothes of some of the stoners. Paul admitted there were many others.

But one day around noon, or mid-day, he saw a bright light from heaven, and he heard a voice. Those who journeyed with him saw the light, but did not hear anything.

The voice spoke to Saul, saying, *"Saul, Saul, why are you forsaking me? Is it hard to kick against the goads?"* When Saul asked, *"Who are you, Lord?"* He answered, *"I am Jesus, whom you are persecuting."*

Saul was delivered, and became a powerful witness for God, his name was changed to Paul. Jesus called him to be a minister, and a witness, right then and there. Apostle Paul, preached in many places, to the Jews and Gentiles, for over twenty years. He had shut up many Christians, in prison for speaking about Christ, now he was shut in prison for speaking out for Christ. Apostle Paul preached, in many places, and wrote many letters, to many churches. To people like

Timothy, and Titus, while being imprisoned in Rome, where he was beheaded. God called him and he spent the rest of his life, preaching and winning souls to Christ.

I just attended a funeral, of a loving, Saint, that I knew. (she was 82). The testimonies she received, let you know, she had done her work over the years. She was a missionary, teacher, and a praying woman, who loved Sunday school. Someone remarked they went to visit her in the hospital, and she ended up praying for them. What a gift she had. What I'm trying to say is, she was a true witness. Even after death, her gifts will live on, in the people her life touched. It makes me ask, "What kind of witness am I?"

I would like for my life to be a influence on others. I will teach the love of God. I will live so others will see Jesus in me. I want to see Jesus' face when I look in the mirror. I want to write about Him as Paul did. I want to leave the works of my Father for others to see. I can't wait for others I have to get about my Father's business. The time that I have left, I will be in the bosom of Christ, and I will be a witness, for the rest of my life.

APOSTLE PAUL

Saul, Saul, why are you persecuting me?
Is what Saul heard him say
This sinner who did not know Christ
Was called by Him that day

His name was changed to Paul
And Paul began a mighty work
He became a preacher sent by God
And he stopped being a jerk

The things he did to the saints
Were now being done to him
They even plotted his death
His future sure looked dim

But God had called him
For a mighty job to do
Although you are imprisoned now
Just know that I'm with you

Apostle Paul started many churches
And he wrote down many things
One day he gave his heart to God
Then he lived for Christ the King

Chapter 19

Shall we continue in sin that grace may abound? (abound; rise in waves; be plentiful). How often in our Christian life, have we met, what I call the rubber band Christian? (Perhaps you are one). A Christian who has been in and out of the church so many times you should be on a rubber band. Taking a chance that God will take you back, when you get ready to come back. That's like playing Russian roulette, with your Christian life.

Our children like to play outside in pleasant weather, but they like to run in for a glass of water, and back outside, run in for the bathroom, and back outside, in to get a toy and back outside, in and out until you find yourself shouting, "Come in and stay or stay outside, in or out you're letting in flies."

It's irritating, as it must be for God, Saints going in and out letting demons in.

It make me wonder if "rubber band" saints have the same spirit in them that I have, now, I didn't always have it, but praise God I know I have it now. You see Jesus gave it to me. It's so sweet and good I want to keep it forever. There is no life outside of Christ that I want more than this, that I want to exchange back and forth, none.

Are you trying Jesus, to see if he will continue to forgive you? Paul wrote in (Romans 6:1) *Shall we continue in sin, that grace may abound?* We know that God's grace is sufficient, and that he gives us new mercies, everyday. Is that why you run in and out so much? You must be pretty sure God will take you back every time. God is slow to anger, but He does get angry. And His punishment is no joke. He told Moses (Rom. 9:15-16) He chooses who He will show mercy, and some of His chosen didn't make it back. Besides the sin that you find so appealing, is but a fleeting moment, compare to life everlasting.

So remember this, you can put your foot in the door, to hold it open so you can get in and out when you want, but one day your foot is going to slip and you will be left outside without a key. Don't take a chance with your Christian life. If you are in and out of Christianity, *you know better.* if God will spew out a luke-warm saint, (Rev. 3:15-16), what will he do to a rubber band aint?

So try to enter the straight and narrow gate for few can find it. (Matt. 7:13-14), *now wide is the gate, and broad is the way to destruction.* Be careful, you don't end up there, on you last trip out.

We are not in this alone, the Holy Spirit, is here to help us. With groaning which cannot be uttered. He makes intercession for us, according to the will of God. You hear Him every time you step backward. You may not want to listen, but you hear Him. He gives us staying power, but you have to want to stay. Paul said in (Rom. 11:22), *consider the goodness and the severity of God.* God do not play!

IN AND OUT

We all need our Lord's grace
To help us run this race
Like being shot like a straight arrow
But a Saint that's in and out
So full of sin and doubt
Needs grace to stay on the straight and narrow

I know this is true
And it depends on you
To always walk with Christ our Lord
If you are luke warm
It will only do you harm
Take this warning and be on guard

This one thing I must say
Remember God don't play
Don't run in and out my friends
The Holy Spirit is here to keep us
Going back and forth is a bust
So let the Holy Spirit keep you in

Chapter 20

Simple Acts of Kindness

I read somewhere that it was *simple acts of kindness week.* a whole week of being devoted to doing kind things for others. A week of helping the handicap, a week of paying the toll for the car behind you in toll booth line, a week of letting the person behind you, in line at the grocery store, with a couple of items go first, a week of letting the car pull into the street ahead of you, or babysitting your neighbors kids so they can have a night out, just little acts of kindness.

Come on now, we as Saints, should be doing these things everyday, right? Well maybe not the baby sitting, with some kids you can only do that once a year, but little things. Even big things if you can. Things that bring a warm felling in your heart and a big reward from heaven. (1 Cor. 3:8).

When Jesus asked for a drink of water at the well, it was a little thing, that's reward was big. Everlasting water. Of course Jesus did acts of kindness everywhere He went.

The men who carried their friend to the house where Jesus was, did an act of kindness when they lowered him through the roof. Their reward was seeing him walk from there. The widow lady did an act of kindness when she fed Elijah, the prophet, her reward was a jar of flour and oil that did not run out, and her sons life.

Maybe these acts of kindness was a little more than paying someones toll fee, but kindness has it's own reward. Don't you feel good all over when you do something for others, and you know it made a difference, to someone? Sure makes me feel good and nobody has to know but me.

Besides there are more than enough people in the world, that are unkind. There are some government jobs where the employee are so unkind, you'd think it was a job requirement. I remember one man that had such a mean look on his face that when he did smile, (with a little coaching from me) he looked as if his face was cracking up into little bitty pieces and falling to the ground. I found out he was a very nice man under that unsmiling face.

When you are saved, the love brings out the kindness. Makes you want to practice it everyday, and not just once a year, in a special week. So work it into your everyday life. It's just another way to say, I love you, to someone. Try to do at least one act of kindness every day, without even thinking about it. Make it a habit, just because you have so much love in your heart.

KINDNESS

It doesn't take much to do
A little act of kindness
Just do it from your heart
What ever you think best

If you can take the time to walk
A grandmother across the street
Or give up your place in line
Well, that would be real sweet

Sometimes an act of kindness
Is just a great big smile
Or maybe a kind word or two
Once in a great while

Go to the hospital if
You can spare the time
You could really help by
Reading to the blind

Just take the time to
Be Christ-like in everything you do
You'll find that an act of kindness
Is just a natural part of you

Chapter 21

One Body

Now there are diversities of gifts, but the same Spirit; and there are differences of administrations, but the same Lord. (1 Cor. 12:4-5).

Each of us are given a different gift, but they all work together to serve the Lord. We have unity, and diversity, in one body. For the body is one, yet it has many members. All the members of that body, are but one, working together, so also is the body of Christ.

I've lived in several places in my lifetime, and so doing I've attended lots of churches, both as a member of my own church and as a visitor to others. I've seen a couple of churches divide, because they couldn't agree on leadership. I've seen a member go else where because, they were passed over for a position, they thought they should be given. Or was told their dress was too short. (when she sat down, the dress completely disappeared).

I saw a church divide, because, the Bishop they elected, the head of the church, didn't get elected, thus a split.

In all the churches that I attended, there was one body. One Pastor, or one head, with an Assistant Pastor or Junior Pastor, but one leader. One Pastors wife, or first lady, (she held that position all by her self, no assistant needed). A choir, (now that's a story all it's own) to many lead singers and not enough back-up). The usher board, the missionary department, the Sunday School, and so on.

All vital parts that make-up the church. What good is a Pastor if he is there by himself? Or an usher, if there is no one to seat? The church needs members to survive. They all need each other in order to work.

Just as our own bodies, need each member. Without eyes we can't see, without ears we can't hear, each part works together, to make us whole.(1 Cor. 12:12-31). Our foot can't be a hand, it is needed for us to walk. Our ears can't be an eye, it is needed for us to hear. Each part has a job to do, and they can't all do the same job.

That church would not have divided if the Bishop, who lost the election, had said, to his followers, "Not this time, but maybe next time," "Everyone can't be the head." That's what he is teaching his flock, right?

Besides we are in this life to serve God, not man. God's number one teaching is *love*. With love you are patient, you don't get mad and leave because things didn't go your way. Love don't work like that. Now if you are being taught against the teachings of God, well it's time to find another teacher. Always let God be the leader, not your own selfishness. Obey God, He's our leader.

DO GOD'S WORK

We are all one body
God needs us one and all
Each part works with the other
To make us all stand tall

Without eyes we cannot see
Or ears we cannot hear
A foot , a hand, a toe
Each part we hold dear

The church needs a whole body
If it's going to work
Deacons, teachers, poets, and preachers
All make up our church

I don't want to hear I
Can't do this or I can't do that
Do what God gave you to do
Or He make take it back

I had to throw poets in there, because I am a poet for Jesus. There are many poets in the churches, that remain silent. I love to recite his Word in rhyme. This is my special blessing.

Chapter 22

The Mirror

Sometime ago, I wrote a poem called "The mirror" it asked when I look into a mirror what do I see? I know what I should see, being a child of God, I should see the face of Christ, looking back at me. When I gave my heart to God, and decided to live this life, my whole aim, was to be Christ-like. To walk in his shoes, well His sandals anyway.

Jesus died for our sins, he left us the Holy Spirit, the Holy Spirit is our guide. The Lord is the Spirit. How can they lead us astray? (2 Cor. 3:17-18) says, *"We are beholding as in a mirror, the glory of the Lord."* We should be seeing in the mirror, a smiling, happy, face, that glows with the goodness of God.

If you always see a grim, unhappy, sad, face, there is something wrong. The Holy Spirit brings joy, not sadness, forgiveness, not meaness, he lifts that old, "I'm always right," feeling and let's you be humble.

I once had a lady, come up to me in a store, and say to me, she had just moved into town, and was looking for a church home, she asked me where I attended. I have to believe that something in my face, told her she was talking to a child of God. If I had been wearing my grouch face, she would have walked on by. Who wants to attend a church where saved people looked like that. I wouldn't. A face like that is not what we get from God. We represent God, whom we *serve*. Everywhere we go, and in everything we do, we should be wearing His face. Everything yall! The World is watching!

So when you look in a mirror, look for Jesus, let Him arise from deep within.

LET GOD ARISE

Let God arise, from deep within
To help us overcome our sins
Let God arise, as we pray
To keep us prayerful through the day

Let God arise, to increase our faith
Make us anxious, Lord I can't wait
Let God arise in everyday life
Make us victorious, in this fight

Arise O Lord, sweet and pure
Let us serve you, we will endure
Let God arise, forever, Lord, forever
Arise in me

Wear Him on your face. Of course if you are not living right, don't look for Him, because He will not be there.

Moses had so much glory, he was all aglow, he had to wear a veil, so the children of Israel couldn't see his glory, only God could. (Exodus 34:29-35).

Remove that veil of unrighteousness, and let the glory of the Lord, shine on your face. Invite Him into your heart, and His love will shine on your face. Get a face-lift, without surgery, let God do it free!

THE MIRROR

When I look into a mirror
What do I see?
Do I see the face of Jesus
Looking back at me?

I see a happy face
With such a sweet glow
A face that only a saved
Holy one would know

Sometimes I see a worried face
With a wrinkled brow
I turn that face upside down
Because Jesus showed me how

Or when the face of greed pops up
From down deep somewhere
I pray to God to remove it
And put generosity there

I pray for a happy face
With a smile so bright
One that tells the whole world
That I am living right

When I look into a mirror
What do I see?
I see the face of Jesus
Smiling back at me

Chapter 23

Let God Do It

I was looking at a TV show the other day, the woman on the show thought she was barren. The changes and the expense, they went through, to get pregnant, nothing worked. Finally they adopted, then after a time she became pregnant. It reminded me of the women in the bible who were barren, and the miracles God gave them.

One was Sarai, Abram's wife. (Gen. 11:30). Sarai took things into her own hands, because of her and her husbands age, she wanted her husband to have a child, so she had her Egyptian maidservant, who's name was Hagar, lay with her husband, so she could conceive of his child. She did. She became pregnant and bore him a son.

Now, Sarai, who's idea it was in the first place, begin to hate Hagar. She treated her so bad, Hagar ran away. Sometimes our great idea's, at least we think they are great at the time, blows up in our faces, don't they? That's because we don't put God in the plan.

Well, God sent an angel, to tell Hagar, to return to her mistress, Sarai, and submit herself to her, because, she was having Abram's first born son. She was to call his name, Ishmael. Abram was then, 86 years old.

Things sure looked dim for Sarai. For it is written; *"Rejoice, O barren, you who do not hear! Break forth and shout you who are not in labor! For the desolate has many more children, than she who has a husband.* (Galations 4:27).

We need to step back, and let God handle things. He promised, Abrams, whom, He renamed Abraham, that his seed shall multiply, for Abraham was to be the father of Nations. God also changed Sarai's name to Sarah.

When she was ninety years old, she conceived. God gave them the promised child, who was named Isaac.

God can do anything, we just have to stay out of His way, and let Him do it. We have let go and let God.

Elizabeth, too, was a barren woman, who too was up in age. (Luke 1:7). Her husband was a priest, called Zacharias. An angel appeared to him,and informed him he was to have a son. A son who was blessed with the Holy Spirit,in his mother's womb. She, of course, gave birth to John the Baptist, who was the forerunner of Jesus Christ.

There is no shame in not giving birth, (I'm not talking of abortion). In (Isa. 54:1), God said, sing and cry aloud. In the forth verse, He says; *be not ashamed, nor disgraced.*

I think the disgrace is woman who choose, career over children, (my opinion, no letters please), and the woman who give birth and throw their children away (a dead baby was found in the trash bin near our house) others have been left on door steps, these are the people who should be shame. There should be lots of shame in those women. That's why I couldn't be God, I couldn't do His job. I'm still trying to be like Him though.

Because of Eve's curse, we bare children in pain, but we rejoice in child birth. I'm sure not being able to concieve is very painful.

Sure Elizabeth, and Sarah was old, when they gave birth, through God's miracles. The older women today may not be giving birth, but there are plenty who are raising their grandchildren, because the birth mothers can't do it, for one reason or another.

So barren women, weep not and rejoice, for God has your reward.

A BARREN WOMAN

There is inside of me an ache
That will not go away
A yearning deep down on the inside
To have a child someday

I want so very much to
Have my very own child
To give birth is what I want
And I've craved it for a while

I feel so empty inside of me
Like I'm just not whole
The years are flying by
Now I feel that I'm too old

I know that God the Father
Is the one who decides
And whether I give birth or not
I will never leave His side

I will live this life He gives me
And never be ashame
I love God and He love me
And He takes away my pain

Chapter 24

David

Remember David, the lad that killed the giant with his sling? He was a man after God's own heart. God loved him. At a young age he was able to do some impossible things, with his sling. He killed a bear and a lion, that were after the sheep that he shepherded. (1Samuel 17:34).

David was described as being, ruddy, beautiful countenance, and goodly to look at. (1 Sam. 16:12), in other words, handsome.

God, through Nathan, anointed him King, because King Saul, had sinned against Him and He turned away from him. (God doesn't stay in an unclean temple). You can't continuingly do wrong, and expect God to stay with you. Anyway, after David slay Goliath, the giant, he was given one of Saul's daughters, as his wife, he became the King's son-in-law. Her name was Michal. King Saul hated David, because the people loved him, and placed him above King Saul. (1 Sam. 18:7-8). Jonathan, Saul's son also loved David, so he told David, that his father, was going to kill him. After King Saul tried to kill him with a spear, David ran.

RUN DAVID RUN

Run David run, Saul is after you
Hide David hide, if he finds you, you're through
I know in your heart he will always be your King
He has a evil spirit in him, that's why he's so mean
Tell me King Saul, for I don't understand
You showed me such love, when I killed the giant man
And as still a boy, it seem that I could do no wrong
Now you want to kill me, now that I am grown
The Lord has delivered you into my hands twice
If I had wanted to I could have taken your life
But you are my King, and you will always be so
Why you want me dead, only you know
So I run and I hide for I am in God's hands
I know I am His chosen, why can't you understand?
Run David Run

His daughter Michal, David's wife, loved David and helped him hide. David remained loyal to King Saul, his King, and although having several chances to kill him, he spared his life.(1 Sam. 24:1-20).

Even later when King Saul, was reported dead to David, he mourned, and wept for both Saul and his son Jonathan, David's friend.

With Saul's death, David became king over all Israel.

David had several wives, besides Michal. Maybe that is why she began to hate David. His wives were, Abgail, widow of Nabal, (she fed David and his army, when her husband refused), and Ahinoam, of Jezreel. There were others. They bore him children.

When the Ark of the Lord, was brought to Jerusalem, there was a big celebration going on. There was sacrifice, music, and dance. David danced with all his might. Michal, who now hated David, her husband, let him have a piece of her mind, about the way he danced. David turned away from her, and she never, bore a child to the day of her death. I think he stopped laying with her. (2 Sam. 6:23).

Michal

Although King David was a mighty warrior
He loved dancing before the Lord
His Music was tambourine, cymbal,
Psalteries, and the harp
When they brought the Ark up
There was shouting and the trumpet blew
Saul's daughter watched David dance
And thought, David I hate you!

After the offering to God, David
Blessed the people then
A cake of bread, a piece of meat, and
A flagon of wine to all the men

Michal, told David he was shameful
Dancing, before the servants that way
And she bore no children at all
Until her dying day

David told Michal, "It's before
The Lord that I play
He chose me to be the ruler
And this I cannot repay
(2 Samuel 6:21-23).

Although he was an anointed King, and God's chosen, he was still
a flesh man. He erred.

One evening, David was walking around, on his roof, he saw a
beautiful, woman bathing, across the way. He asked and found out
her name was Bathsheba, and she was the wife of Uriah, the Hittite.
David, with all the wives he had already, he had to have her. He send
for her and lay with her. She became pregnant. Her husband was away,
fighting with King David's army. He brought him home, to cover his
sin, by having her husband lay with her. Her husband didn't do as

David planned, he did not go home. He slept at the King's servants house instead.(the best laid plans…) so David had to come up with another. He had him sent to the front line, into the worst part of the battle, so he could be killed, and he was.

After a period of mourning, Bathsheba and David were married. King David, who was God's chosen, sinned, against Him. God was displeased, he sent Nathan to David with a message.

Thou Art The Man

Who shall take a man's only ewe
When he has so many?
And never even think about
The fact that he has plenty

Nathan told David
Don't you understand?
You have done this thing
David, thou art the man

God has given you so much
Riches for all your life
That was not enough for you
You stole another man's wife

Not only did you steal her
You had her husband killed
To do such an awful thing
Was truly not God's will

Because of the sin you did
Your baby son will die
Thou art the man David
You are the reason why

Read all about King David in the books of 1ˢᵗ and 2ⁿᵈ Samuel. God blessed the seed of their union, he was King Solomon, a wise man, indeed, he was.

Chapter 25

Easter

Man has turned this day into
Easter rabbits and dyed eggs
And forgotten all about Jesus
Rising from the tomb, where He was laid

We try hard not to think
Of our Saviour on the cross
The son of God who gave His life
So our souls would not be lost

The Word who was made flesh
Was tortured and He was beat
He gave His life for mankind
Who's not worthy to kiss His feet

This wonderful man of innocence
With a thief on both His sides
Said; "It is finished," and then
Gave up the ghost, and died

Now wait a minute, it's not over
That's why we have this day
Our God sent an angel
And he rolled the stone away

Now ask yourself about His love
And about His loving grace
Jesus died upon the cross that day
To save the human race

Today is Tuesday, a couple of days after Easter Sunday. Easter Sunday is the day we celebrate that Christ rose from the grave. On Friday, or three days before, he was nailed to the cross, he gave His life for our sins. He was buried, He was placed in Joesph's tomb, with a hugh rock blocking the entrance, with guards placed there so no one could come and steal His body.

The grave couldn't hold the only begotten Son of God. On the third day He was gone. He had arisen.

But Easter week-end is over why am I talking about it on Tuesday? Well, because, what Jesus did for mankind, was much too big to hold it to three days. You can celebrate your dyed eggs and bunny rabbits three days, but Jesus' sacifice should be remembered the whole year, and not with baby chicks, rabbits, and dyed eggs.

Now I'm not saying you should not, have them, it's fun for the kids, to have Easter egg hunts (I enjoy watching them), we dress them up in suits and ties, frills and hats, (there are some cities where they have parades), then the whole family goes to church once a year. True very true, only once a year. But when they get to church, they should be taught, the real meaning of Easter day.

They should be taught, Jesus, the son of God, was made flesh, and was born into a world of sin. Born to die for the sins of man. God loves man, and He continually, gives us a way out of sin. Thank-you Jesus!

He sent to us, Jeremiah, but many rebelled, He sent Ezekiel, to a rebellious people, (Ezek.2:7). God sent many Prophets, (He's still sending them), to His hard-headed people, (still hard-headed), some even told of the coming of Christ, but man rebelled.

God *loves* us so much! *God so loved the world that, He sent His only begotten Son, that we could have everlasting life,* (John3:16). (John 1:4), tells us that *the Word became flesh, the Word became Jesus Christ,* a flesh and blood man. A man with a family, his father was Joesph, a carpenter, his mother, Mary, a virgin when she had Him, and he had brothers and sisters too. One brother was James who wrote the book of James.

Jesus had a job to do here on Earth, for His Father, who art in Heaven, to teach us sinners, God's Word. He walked around telling the good news, while He gathered his disciples. Crowds gathered where ever He walked, to heard the Word and see the miracles.

He gave sight to the blind, he healed the lame, he raised the dead, He wept, he taught of God's great love for us. He told of living waters, that springs into everlasting life, all we have to do is believe.

So Easter week-end is really when the flesh life came to an end. His death on the cross, not an easy death, he was beaten, cursed, belittled, and tortured. A death, where they cast lots for his garments. A death that made his flesh body, call out, *"Father, why has thou forsaken me?"* (Mark 15:34). A death when the sun refused to shine, (Luke 23:44-45), where the tomb couldn't hold the body, Jesus arose. He is risen, (Luke 24:1-12). The good news is we can, and should celebrate, not just on Easter, but the whole year round. Praise God, He is risen.

He Went Home

He hung on the cross that awful day
Soldiers gambled on his clothes
A crown of thorns was on his head
How he suffered, he alone knows

With nails in his hands he hung there
His company was two thieves
One thief only taunted him
While the other cried "Lord please?"

When we think of how He suffered
The pain He bore for sin
My Lord Jesus suffered
And died for all men

Jesus cried out and yielded up His spirit

The Earthquake shook
And graves opened too
Truly this was the son of God
Said the guards, for they then knew

Jesus was buried in Joesph's new tomb
But on the third day he was gone
I never get tired of telling this
My Lord, Saviour, He went home

Chapter 26

When I was a kid, (talk about the olden days), I remember in youth class, at church, we would play, King and Queen of the chair. You would ask questions, and if the person in the chair couldn't answer, you became the Queen or King. You always had to prove your answer with scripture.

One popular question was "Who was the oldest man in the Bible?"

The answer was of course, *Methuselah*.

You see before the flood, men, begotten from Adam, lived long lives. Adam, himself, lived nine-hundred thirty years, his son Seth, lived nine-hundred twenty years, and so on down the line, to Methuselah, who was nine-hunderd, sixty-nine years, when he died. Methuselah, begot a son named Jared, who begot Enoch, a true man of God, who begot a son, until Lemech, who was the father of Noah.

By the time of Noah, the world had become an evil place. The sons of God, saw the daughters of man and mated with them. Their off-spring were mighty men. (Gen.6:4). There were giants on the Earth. Evil and wickedness was a bound.

God was sorry He made man. We seem to have a natural ability to make God sorry He made us. This time He decided to destroy his creation, man, beast, and fowl. God found favor in Noah, who was a just and perfect man, who walked with God.(Gen. 6:8-9). We know the story of Noah, and how he built the ark, took aboard the animals, his wife and sons and their wives, and lived to replenish the Earth. Well, Noah lived 950 years.

After the flood, man's years got less and less. Shem, his son, lived 600 years. Abraham, on down the line, lived 175 years, Jacob lived 147, and Joseph 110.

There are people today, that have live over 100 years. We seem to be living longer today, than a few decades back. I don't think Methuselah's record will ever be broken, in our time, but Joesph's has already been passed.

Now you may live to be 100 or more, one of my aunts is 100 and a ½(as the kids like to point out). It is possible, however you just may not make it. So whether you be 10, 40, 60, or 80, I encourage you to live each year, in God's favor, so you can really live after you die.

METHUSELAH

It's hard to imagine living
So many, many, years
Like the men before the flood
Over nine hundred don't you hear

Methuselah who was the oldest man
Was nine hundred sixty-nine
And people call you old at sixty
In this day and time

We celebrate each year we have
At our birthday parties
Trying not to tell our age
After we turn forty

What good is longevity if you
Do nothing with that life
If you spend all those years
Living long with out Christ

Chapter 27

Abram and Sarai

Abram told Sarai, "When we get there
Pretend you're not my wife"
"A woman of your beauty
Could cause the men to take my life"

Just tell them when they ask you
You are indeed my sister, dear
Then we can pass through their land
Without you shedding a single tear

But Pharaoh found favor in
Her beauty, which was fair
He paid Abram lots of kindness
So he could keep her there

But God did not approve
Of Abram's silly plan
He sent plagues on Pharoah's house
So he send them from his land

Why didn't you just tell us
That this beauty was your wife?
You could have told the truth
You didn't have to hide

This is a story of a man, who had a beautiful wife. This was a traveling man, sent by God, looking for a new place to live. In his travels, he was to pass through a land, where the men, would, maybe, kill him, if they found favor in his wife. So he had a plan.

He would pass his wife off as his sister, (she really was his half sister), then he would live. His plan worked beautifully. But his beautiful wife (sister) was found favorable there and he received many gifts and riches, from Pharaoh.

This man was Abram and the beautiful wife was Sarai. God had already found favor in Abram and although Sarai was barren, He had blessed their seed. (Gen. 12:3-7).

So Abram had a plan, it was not God's plan, so God sent plague to the Pharaoh's house, because of Sarai, being there. Pharoah sent them away, saying, "Why didn't you tell us she was your wife, and not your sister?"

Abram left with his wife, and all the riches, that he had been given. There is a word for what he did, is it not? Well, Abram was a blessed man, but yet a man, and man's plans are not always God's plans.

Even today, we come up with what we really think, is a good plan. One that can't miss. Then when it goes astray, we realize, God was not in it. Now you may be wondering, how can God, help us to make plans? He's not even here. Well my friend, He is here! If you listen you can hear Him talk to you.

Pray about things, fast about things, and *wait* on an answer. Use that saying, that was real popular awhile back, *"What would Jesus do?"* It still works. It's a real good way of making decisions, and what a good way to live your life everyday. Trying to be like Jesus, in all things. Listen! You will hear Him. Believe, you will feel Him. Believe that God can do anything, because He can do anything, if the plan is His and not ours.

We must learn to obey God, in all things. Take for instance, Abraham, (God changed his and Sarah's names), who was old when Isaac was born. So was Sarah, his wife. Isaac was their only child, (Abraham had others). God told Abraham to take Isaac on a trip to offer him as a burnt offering, as a sacrifice to Him. (The Lord will test us from time to time). Can you stand the test? Abraham took Isaac, and all he needed for the burnt offering, and went where he was told to go.

As he lay the wood on Isaac, and drew back the knife, to kill him, God stopped him. He then provided a ram stuck in a bush, for him to use instead.(Gen. 22:13). Trust God, He always has a ram in the bush.

Sarah died at 127 years old. Abraham, lived not only, long enough to see Isaac marry, he remarried, and had several more children. As God promised, his seed was plenty on Earth. From his seed, Isaac, eventually came Jesus, our Savior.

Abraham's seed

When Isaac first met Rebekah
Was it love at first sight?
God had chose a bride for him
God always does what's right

Isaac born of Abraham was
Blessed and all his seed
Abraham could die in peace
Knowing he had done his deed

Don't forget about Ishmael for
He was Abraham's son too
He had a special blessing on his life
then one nation became two

Although, Ishmael's family multiplied
It seem Rebekah could not conceive
Isaac prayed and ask the Lord
God blessed them with sons indeed

Rebekah gave birth to twins
That were different as day and night
Jacob being mild dwell in the tent
While Esau lived by his might

Chapter 28

Offering and Sacrifices

Moses

I Am, told Moses to set His people free
Go down into Egypt there is where they'll be
Go and tell Pharoah it's time to give them up
Don't be afraid to tell him, he'd just better duck

Go! Take Aaron and I will have your back
My signs and wonders will show them, just where I'm at
Water will become blood, then frogs, lice, and flies
Diseases, boils, and locusts, until his first born dies

Lead my children Moses, through the Red Sea
And on the land
Milk and honey awaits you
You can do it, I said you can

Come into the mountain
Come Moses you and I
I will give you ten commandments
Laws they must live by

I didn't ask you to obey my laws
This is what I command
He gave these laws to Moses
To be followed by every clan

He taught both Moses and brother Aaron
Just how to do the sacrifice
Only the blessed ones could do them
And they had to do them right

When the bull was burnt, on the altar, the Lord had a sweet aroma, that He likes. Next time you are BBQing and the smell is drifting up, think of this.

When the laws were given to Moses, the laws of priesthood, were given to both Moses and Aaron, his brother. One duty was to offer sacrifices, unto the Lord. Only the Priest could perform them, and only in certain ways. Two of Aaron's son were burned to death, because they performed them the wrong way, displeasing God.

They had to offer the sacrifices, to the Lord, for the people as well as themselves. One was called a **Burnt Offering**, or burnt sacrifice. The burnt sacrifice was to be of a unblemished male animal, to offer a sweet aroma to the Lord.

Then there was the **Grain Offering**, it was to be of fine flour, with anointed oil and frankincense poured on it. It too was burnt, to send a sweet aroma to the Lord. Everything we have comes from God, some of every thing was offered back to Him in appreciation. First fruit, was included in this offering.

The **Peace Offering**, or the **Freewill Offering**, was usually for a special thank-you or a vow of praise, for God's goodness, in giving so much. An animal was usually used. The **Sin Offering**, was a young unblemished bull, the priest offered in burnt sacrifice unto the Lord to atone for sin, and the sin would be forgiven. Sin must be dealt with quickly, before it could spread.

The **Trespass Offering**, a person guilty of touching an unclean thing, or bore the guilt of hearing a spoken oath, or speaks evil and swears, he bears the guilt and must offer a trespass offering. All offerings must be the very best of animal or grain. This offering is *most* holy.

The Bible also mentions the **Wave Offering** and the **Heave Offering,** you'll find them in the book of Leviticus.

Jesus, the Son of God, was sent to Earth as flesh so that sacrifice would no longer be necessary. (Eph. 5:2), says, *Jesus' death on the cross was a offering and sacrifice of sweet aroma, to God.* Only the shedding of His blood can forgive sin. (Heb. 9:22). Christ's blood was the fulfillment of God's will. His sacrifice, of death, on the cross wiped out burnt offerings. By the blood of Jesus Christ, we can atone for every sin. (Heb. 10:1-10).

Now does that mean, because of the death of Christ, on the cross, we no longer have to keep the Commandments of God as well? They were given to Moses about the same time. Let's review them again.

The greatest of all: **I am the Lord thy God, thy shall have no other god before Me.** in (Deut. 5:8), it says *you shall not carve any likeness of anything in heaven above, or on the Earth beneath for worship.* So should we be praying to statues of Christ on the cross, or likenesses of the virgin Mary, who after Jesus was born became a wife and mother, she is no longer a virgin, especially since we don't know what they looked like except there're created in God's image? Or any graven images? Be careful Saints, God is a jealous God. His mercy will be shown on those who keep His Commandments.

Don't take the Lord's name in vain.

Keep the Sabbath day Holy. To many Saints, that a joke. Unfortunally, some bread winners, have no chose, but to work on Sunday, (Our Sabbath), but those who wait until Sunday morning to wash the car, or clean the house, or cook a big meal, remember the Sabbath is all day. There was a time when all ironing, washing , cooking, had to be done on Saturday night, so no work was done on Sunday. We are not even teaching this any more. What ever day you observe as the Sabbath, keep it holy, all day, it's God's command.

Honor thy Father and thy Mother. this commandment give us longevity, if we obey. (Eph. 6:1-3).

Do not kill

Do not commit adultery that's one sin that deserve a chapter all by it's self. Some preachers thinks it wasn't talking to them. Wise up before some sweet, young thing, takes you straight to hell. Young people fornication, is included in this commandment. All sex when you are not married is <u>sin.</u>

Do not Steal

Do not bear false witness. Don't lie period. Don't make your family lie. If you are home answer the phone. Don't say you will be there or do that and never show up, don't make promises, you can't keep. Do not lie on someone for personal gain, or any other reason.

Do not covet your neighbor's wife, or his belongings. the grass is not greener on the other side of the fence. (well my neighbor's is, how do she do it, I water). Just be thankful you have your side and praise God for having them. (wife or husband).

God is love, and with love in us, we can live a wonderful life, here on Earth, and an even better one in Heaven, after we die. I'm going, hope to see you there.

Chapter 29

I have a new Kings James study Bible, that I love. I have used it so much that it is worn and marked. I also like using my mothers, King James Bible. (I think I'll have to retire it soon though, because mama wore it out), it has many marked pages, and all through it, are writing in the margins, and on the sides and bottom. It makes me feel as if I can see her special places she liked to go.

She was a minister, and unfortually, for me, I never got to hear her preach much, I was to busy sinning. I also lived in a different town, some miles away. But her Bible lets me go in my head, to where she might have went. It engulf me and takes me to a warm place.

Reading the stories of the Bible, still excites me, over and over again. For instance, reading the story of Joseph, over again for the I don't know how manyeth time, (that should confuse the spell check), I still can't hardly wait to get to the part where he tells his brothers who he is? Love it just love it.

I have teared up, yes I cry at sad movies, and happy ones too. And I still want to punish the woman who lied on him. See, I couldn't do God's job.

In books written by man, when they make them into movies they change things to how they want them to end. Even the Bible stories are changed, but God's Word never changes. I may want to punish the woman but God has other plans. It was God's will for him to go to prision.

I also like the part where, as a child he was his father's favorite son. His father doted over him. He made him a coat of many colors, that part reminds me, of my baby brother, he to was the favorite, and got special treatment. I can see Joseph running to tell on his older brothers. We had one of those too. My little sister was going to tell it, if it killed her. (she got many threats but she survived). I remember one of mom's birthdays, we cooked a special meal, baked a cake, even scrapped up enough money, to buy her a gift,(we were poor, with eight kids) to surprise her after got off work. She had to walk about two blocks from where her ride dropped her off.

Then I noticed baby girl was missing. Sure enough, we looked out the window, and there she was running to get to mom, to tell. She did. Mom enjoyed the birthday even though, she wasn't surprised. We lost my little sister a couple of years ago, to cancer. I really miss her. (Give to cancer research, help wipe it out.)

Back to Joseph, one of mom's scriptures she marked was (Isaiah 55:6-9), *seek ye the Lord while He may be found. Call upon Him while He is near.* and in the eighth verse it says; *for your though are not my thoughts; neither are your ways my ways.* God plans ahead, he already knew, what Joseph's life would be, from the day of his birth. What I would have done don't even matter. He could handle it without my help. Sometimes what we thing is a good idea, is not all that good. (sorry to burst your bubble). We have first and foremost, to follow God's ways. He will lead us, by the Holy Spirit, the right way. There's only one way, and it's God's way.

Joseph

Joesph as a boy was without
A doubt, his father's favorite
He ran around doing this and that
While his older brothers labored

His dad made him a special coat
And it had many colors
He ran around flunting it
Before his jealous older brothers

Then he started having dreams
That made him above the rest
His brothers really go mad and
Thought killing him would be best

Rueben saved his life that day
And they threw him in a hole
I cannot kill my brother, said he
If the truth be told

They sold Joesph to a carvan
And told his father he was dead
Don't feel bad for Joseph though
His destiny lies ahead

Read about Joseph and his family in the book of Genesis 37-50.

Chapter 30

Blessed are the pure in heart for they shall see God. (Matt. 5:8).

Pure; to be pure is to be, clean, modest, undefiled, moral, without blemish or fault.

That's a lot to fit into such a little word. Just how can a person be expected to live everyday, and yet remain all of that? If we are called the children of God, *we must be purified, just as He is pure.* (1 John 3:2-3). He will abide in us if we are pure, for He will not live in a unclean temple. Therefore we must make changes in our hearts, when we invite Him to come in. You see He only comes when we invite Him. I can't invite Him into your heart, although I would like to go around putting Him in everyone I know, but I can't, only you can, let Him in yours. He will not stay if your heart is not pure. You have to get rid of sin and keep it out.

Satan tries to creep back in with unclean thoughts, with his what if this? And what if that's? He tries to creep into your prayers, into your actions, even into what you wear. That's right what you wear can cause, unpure thoughts in others. And I'm talking about both men and women. Satan will send you things of the world, but worldly things can cause you to lose God. *Do not love the world, or the things of the world.* (1John 2:15-17). These things are but a moment, a life in Christ is everlasting.

Quite frankly, I can live without, lust, greed, pride, envy, and other material things. I find a life in Christ in me so rewarding, I don't need anything else. You know, He just keeps on giving me things, just because,he wants me to have them. Ain't God good?

Now we have to *beware of the spirits, all are not God!* (1John 4:7-8). There are false prophets, that claim to be of God, and will lead you straight to hell. This is the spirit of the anti-Christ. He is here on the

Earth, seeking whom he may devour. Test the spirits, you'll know God, through love. (1 John 4:7-8).

Keeping a pure, loving heart, and being God's servant, is pure joy, and I wouldn't have it any other way. I intend to see God. That's how I will live my life.

PURE OF HEART

Blessed are the pure in heart
For they shall see God's face
Keeping a pure heart is the only way
That we can win this race

Beware of the unclean spirits
All spirits are not the Lord's
If you let the wrong one in
Beware you can fall real hard

Living without greed, pride,and lust
And other material things
Does not make me feel sad at all
But makes my heart gleem

I gave my heart to God with love
And I intend to keep it pure
Walking always in His footsteps
Of that you can be sure

What kind of spirit is in you?
What kind of spirit is in you?
Only you can tell
Is it the spirit of God and love
Or the one that'll take you to hell?

Do you have the spirit that on
Sundays you jump and shout
But you really want to be elsewhere
And can't wait till church is out

God's Holy Spirit is one that
Makes you love one another
You have so much love for everyone
As if they were your mother

You no longer feel hateful
Or no longer want revenge
You have a loving spirit that
Makes you love all women and men

So look in your heart
Check the spirit that is there
Always keep a pure spirit of love
It'll take you anywhere

Chapter 31

I have been reading the Bible, from cover to cover, as so many of us do. This is my first time finishing it. I've started several times, and never finished, but now I am in Revelations. (p.s. I finished).

I don't know why, but Revelations always used to scare me. Before it was always gloom and doom to me. Now, the the help of the Holy Spirit in me, I have a new revelation about Revelations.

It's pretty much a raod map to Heaven or to Hell. It's up to you to decide, which road to take. One is broad the other is narrow. God has given us the golden rules, and He expects us to live by them.

Satan, is loose, and he's constantly changing his rules. He has stuff going on today, that our grandfathers, wouldn't believe could be done. And it is evil! It's sad to say but you saps are falling them, right and left. (I did too once), but his rules are taking you straight to hell. If you have an ear, you'd better listen to what the word has to say. (Rev. 2:7).

FIGHT THE BATTLE

Pray without ceasing
Put the whole armor on
God leads us into battle
He will not leave us alone

You don't need guns and knifes
Or no such things as these
You need to call on Jesus
Call Him from down on your knees

He gives us the Holy Spirit
Along with peace, joy, and love
With the fruit of the spirit in us
We can be gentle as a dove

God makes us ready for the battle
Now, we must get ready for the fight
The devil will come after us
We must fight him with all our might

I recently, lost a nephew to violence, maybe I should say another nephew, or cousin. (there has been quite a few in our family), and our only comfort is, maybe they had time to ask for forgiveness, before death, and God forgave them. God has been known to not hear you.

GOD WOULD NOT HEAR

When you fasted and mourned in the fifth
And seventh month, was it for Me?
When you did not eat, and did not drink
Was it for me, or was it for thee?

You have refused to listen and
Have closed your ears to hear
You have made your hearts like stone
To the law, and show no fear

You have not heeded to the prophets
That God has sent to you
Therefore came His great wrath
Now He has closed His ears too

Therefore there came a time that
He cried and you would not hear
When you cried to the Lord of Hosts
He would not hear, and scattered you from there

He wants everyone on Earth to serve Him, not do all the evil you
can do, and on your dying bed, your last words are, "Lord forgive me."
You are taking a chance that He will. He created us to serve Him. He
sent Prophets to warn us, then when we didn't get it right, He sent
Jesus, to die for us. Jesus, His only begotten son, to show us the way.
We are cleansed by the blood, but the world is more sinful, now then
ever before. Sinners are falling by the wayside, Saints are falling by the
wayside, preachers that have been leaders for years are falling by the
wayside. A broad road to destruction. Look out for the thief.

THE THIEF

The devil will steal your blessing
If you let him, and O, he's going to try
While God is giving you blessings
ole Satan is standing by

All he needs is a opening
And he will slip right in
Take your mind off the Savior
Is what that devil intends

"You can't keep your mind on Jesus"
Are things he like to say
"It's impossible to stay prayerful
No one can do it, no way!"

Alittle lie here and a little sin there
A little is all you need
Just give me a little opening
And I can plant my seed

Yes, satan will steal your blessings
Saints, you'd better watch out
Keep your mind ever prayerful
And stay clear of that lout
Therefore it came to pass, that as He cried, and they would not hear; so they cried
and I would not hear, said the Lord of host (Zech. 7:14)

Why are we so weak? Is what the devil is offering so appealing, that you will trade a life with Christ, to burn in hell? Satan is mad at us, Saints, and he is coming at us in full force. We had better stand tall, with God's whole armor on, or you may find yourself in the pit that is enlarging itself, to hold all of you. All who reject Christ, live there. (Rev. 9: 1-19). Woe to you!

WOE TO YOU HYPOCRITES

Woe to you hypocrites, you shut
The door of Heaven against men
You won't go in yourselves, and
You keep others from entering in

Woe to you hypocrites, you
Pretend with long prayer
You will receive condemnation
For there's no truthfulness there

Woe to you hypocrites, you pay
Tithes that matter not
You omit justice, mercy,and faith
You know this makes God hot

Woe to you hypocrites, on the outside
You appear white as snow
But on the inside, well,
Only you and God knows

Woe to you hypocrites, you'd
Better get it right, and do it now
So if God forgives you
To Him you will bow

Woe; great sorrow, grief, trouble
Woeful; full of woe, sad, causing woe, pitiful, wretched.

Hypocrite; one who pretends to be pious, virtuous, without really being, pretending to be what one is not.

My, my, my, my, my! What a sad person to be. This is what Jesus called the Scribes, and Pharisees, when he was speaking to the multitude, and to His disciples. The Scribes were good for asking Jesus questions, that they thought would trip Him up. The Bible says they sat on Moses seat, (Remember Moses' mercy seat?), and gave orders for the people to observe, but didn't observe them themselves.

They do to be seen. You know, always sitting on the front row, Sunday morning, in fine array, but you never see them at prayer meetings or Bible study. They expect praise for any work they do or say. "Not so hypocrite," Jesus said. *"He who exalts himself will be humbled, and he who humbles himself, will be exalted."* (Matt. 23:12).

Exalt means to raise in status dignity; to praise dignity; to fill with joy, and pride, etc. In other words, he who is on his high horse, will be brought down to the humble, and the humble will be placed on high.

A hypocrite, is only pretending to have what he doesn't have in the first place. Woe to you hypocrite! Open your eyes, Saints. Are you causing someone not to reach the kingdom of Heaven, by your actions? Are your prayers long, and empty? Are you blind and yet trying to lead the blind? You'd better wake up! Your sin is even greater than, when you harm one of God's little ones. Besides, how can you walk the straight and narrow path, when you can't see where you are going?

It's time to look within our selves. Nobody wants to be a hypocrite, not on purpose, I don't think. Can you imagine people walking up to you and saying, "How do you do, sister hypocrite" or "Morning, brother, hypocrite?" It would upset us would it not? Well, don't live so anyone, can think it, or say it behind your back. If you do woe to you, hypocrite.

The end

Look for coming soon, a new book
"Through the Bible in Rhyme"
By Merlene Howard

CPSIA information can be obtained
at www.ICGtesting.com
Printed in the USA
JSHW020017270523
42341JS00002B/103

9 781420 890037